GOLF

MERRILL D. HARDY
ELEANOR A. WALSH
California State University, Northridge

GOODYEAR PHYSICAL ACTIVITIES SERIES
EDITED BY J. TILLMAN HALL

Goodyear Publishing Company, Inc.
Santa Monica, California 90401

Library of Congress Cataloging in Publication Data

Hardy, Merrill D.
  Golf.

  (Goodyear physical activities series)
  Bibliography: p. 112
  1. Golf.   I. Walsh, Eleanor A., joint author.   II. Title.
GV965.H27 1980   796.352'3   79-22752
ISBN 0-87620-353-5

GOLF
Merrill D. Hardy
Eleanor A. Walsh

Copyright © 1980
GOODYEAR PUBLISHING COMPANY
Santa Monica, California 90401

Current printing (last digit):
10 9 8 7 6 5 4 3 2 1
Y-3535-5
Printed in the United States of America

ACKNOWLEDGMENTS

We wish to express our sincere appreciation and gratitude to Dr. Judy Brame, who is responsible for the photography in the book; to Dr. Ann Stutts for the illustrated materials; to Maureen Petry Hosp and Doug Robbins, PGA Professional, who served as models for the pictures; and to Larry Krock, who contributed material for the chapter on "Conditioning." Finally, we express a special thanks to Rosemary Huttner for assisting in the typing, and to Kathy Seacord, who prepared the final manuscript.

CONTENTS

EDITOR'S NOTE

The Goodyear Publishing Company is most pleased to have Dr. Merrill Hardy and Dr. Eleanor Walsh combine their knowledge in the writing of this book. Both authors are professors of physical education at California State University, Northridge. They have had extensive experience in teaching, coaching and playing this fascinating and challenging sport.

Interesting and informative facts about golf history, selection of equipment, and the characteristics of the game in general are presented in the first chapter. Then the basic fundamentals of the golf swing are carefully described, illustrated and summarized through each step. The reader is guided through technique and strategy with woods, irons and putting; each discussion is summarized with the handy "technique check points." All aspects of the game are covered—the long game, the short game, the trouble shots. A very useful discussion of etiquette and the important rules of golf is also included.

But, regardless of how far or how well you can hit the ball, unless you have mastered the information on the mental aspects of the game, you will probably never achieve optimum enjoyment in golf. A full chapter on the mental aspects of golf stresses the importance of this often neglected topic. There is also a detailed chapter on correcting common errors. Each problem is described, the cause analyzed, and a corrective technique indicated.

The final portion of the book contains ideas about practice, strategy, and conditioning, helpfully illustrated with photographs. The book concludes with a complete glossary of golfing terminology.

I have played golf for many years, read lots of literature on the sport, and observed numerous scratch golfers demonstrate their skills—this book provides a clear, accurate and latest "state of the art" description of the fundamentals of golf. Read it carefully. You will find it most rewarding.

BIOGRAPHY

Merrill D. Hardy has taught golf in high school and college for 25 years—and has played the sport for over 30 years. He is currently Professor of Physical Education at California State University, Northridge. He received his Ph.D. at the University of Southern California.

Eleanor A. Walsh is Professor and Coordinator of the Undergraduate Physical Education Program at California State University, Northridge, where she also serves as Women's Golf Coach. She holds a Ph.D. in physical education from the University of Southern California, and is a former President of the Southwest District of the American Alliance for Health, Physical Education, Recreation, and Dance.

GOLF

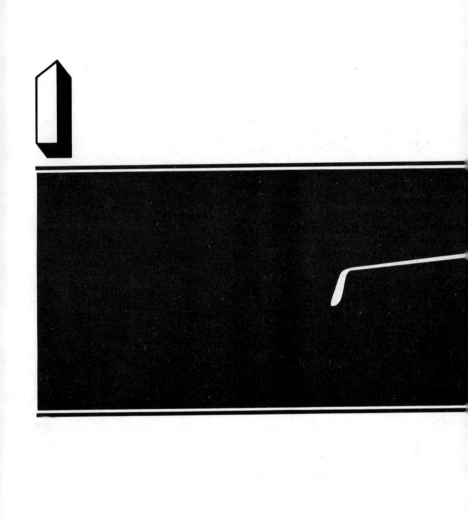

INTRODUCTION TO GOLF

The object of a round of golf is for the player to hit a ball from a teeing area and eventually to stroke it into a small hole on a putting green in the least number of strokes possible. Various clubs may be used to stroke the ball. There are eighteen different holes on a golf course (some courses have nine holes) varying in length from 100 to 600 yards. In a description of the game such as the foregoing, a round of golf sounds quite easy. But as any golfer can tell you, golf is one of the most challenging games in sport today. Its popularity is widespread and you need not look far to see fine golf tournaments on television and in your local area and to read about various aspects of golf in newspapers, magazines, and books. No doubt the growth of professional golf and the extensive television coverage have inspired and motivated more and more people to play this fascinating game.

WHERE DID GOLF COME FROM?

Although it is difficult to trace the beginning of golf, apparently the first version of something like golf was engaged in by Scottish shepherds thousands of years ago when they struck pebbles with their crooks and tried to knock them into holes in the ground. According to legend, they competed with each other for both distance and accuracy. Other early stories say that golf originated in Holland and still others credit France with a game like golf centuries ago. However, the game which is close to what we play today originated in Scotland. In the fifteenth century King James II prohibited golf because it was detracting from the skill of archery, and at that time the defense of the country depended upon expertise with the bow and arrow. When King James IV became interested in playing golf in the early 1500s, opposition to the game gradually disappeared.

Many golf groups and organizations began to appear, and the first woman golfer was Mary, Queen of Scots. Golf continued to grow in popularity. The St. Andrews Society of Golfers was organized in the mid-1700s, and in 1884 became the famous Royal and Ancient Golf Club of St. Andrews. The St. Andrews course originally had twenty-two holes. For a long time the golfers played eleven holes in a straight line and then repeated ten of those holes plus one other hole near the beginning of the course. Later the decision was made to stabilize the round at eighteen holes. The start of modern-day tournaments was the British Open, which was held in 1860, followed by the British Amateur Tournament twenty-five years later.

Golf was introduced in the United States in 1888 by a Scot named John Reid. Reid played the game with his neighbors on a three-hole course, and they shared a single set of golf clubs. In the early days in America the number of holes played often varied from five to six, but as the popularity of the game grew, additional holes were added. Two of the first golf courses in the United States were Shinnecock Hills on Long Island and the Chicago Golf Club. The site of the first eighteen-hole golf course in the United States is not definitely known, but Blair MacDonald, an American who had gone to school in St. Andrews, enlarged the Chicago Course from nine to eighteen holes in the late nineteenth century. Just before the turn of the twentieth century, the first public golf links were built in New York City, and from then on golf became a sport available to all classes of people, not just a game for the rich.

In 1895 the USGA (United States Golf Association) Open was established, but it was not until 1911 that an American, Johnny McDermott, won the tournament. Since those early days the growth of golf for amateurs and professionals of both sexes has been amazing. Not only major cities but small towns have public and private courses which attract millions of golfers at every level of skill.

WHY PLAY GOLF?

Why do so many people of all ages play golf? Of what value is it to follow a little white ball around a golf course? Sometimes even the highly skilled golfer, in a moment of extreme frustration over a bad shot or a poor round, asks these questions. But even the most discouraged golfer forgets quickly and is drawn back to this intensely interesting, challenging game almost as though he were hypnotized by it. Probably the reason given most frequently by people who play golf is that the game is fun. Granted, for some who play the game it is not fun but almost like work, and it seems to produce, rather than relieve, stress. Those who approach golf with this attitude should find something else to do, because it is only a game and it should be enjoyed. Even Jack Nicklaus, probably the most outstanding professional of our time, keeps golf in the perspective of a game and does not place too high a priority on a bad round. As with any game involving skill, you may not like it immediately until a reasonable level of proficiency is developed. But golf is one of those games that can really "take hold" and can become an important part of your leisure time, both as a player and as a spectator.

One of the many advantages of golf is that it can be played alone or with one, two, or three other people in a group. You can enjoy the sociability of friends as you compete against them and the course. It is one of the only sports in which you can engage in some conversation between shots and still not detract from the game. Golf also has a simple system of handicapping which can equalize competition between players of different abilities in the same playing group and make it fair and fun for everyone.

Although you may not consciously set out to play golf because of the values it affords overall health, many potential benefits are definitely possible. Those who are able to walk the course as they play derive good physical exercise. Also of great importance in our tense and fast-paced society are the mental-health benefits of relaxing and becoming involved in an activity apart from the stress of the regular job. The aesthetic and emotional satisfactions of being outside in the beautiful surroundings of a golf course as well as the emotional experience of feeling a shot that was hit just right are vital contributions to a person's well-being.

Another advantage of golf is that you can truly play it for a lifetime. Those who can't walk the course may use motorized cars so that they can still experience the exhilaration and pleasure of a round of golf. There are thousands of physically handicapped golfers who play the game well. It is obvious from observing people who play golf that there are no particular size characteristics which are necessary: the slightly built and short person can be just as adept as the larger individual. In fact, sometimes the larger and stronger person tries to "muscle" his way through the game and finds out very quickly that this is ineffective.

One of the main challenges golf offers is that even when you're playing with other players, you must play the whole game and the whole course yourself. The responsibility and pressure are completely on the individual. No one can cover a shot for you; you must play each stroke yourself. It has often been said that golf is a very humbling game and a great character builder, for you must face and cope with all situations on your own. Every shot is different, every course is different, and each time you play you have a new experience. It is definitely not a game for the person who gives up easily, but even one or two good shots will keep you coming back. No one has ever totally mastered the game, and probably no one ever will, but once you start playing you're likely to join the millions of others who think there's nothing like golf.

GOLF EQUIPMENT

Once you become interested in golf, your next step is to purchase some equipment. You will gain more satisfaction from the game when you have selected equipment which meets your own abilities and

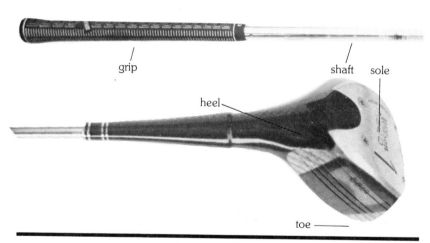

Figure 1.1 *Parts of the club.*

preferences and which is available any time you have a chance to play golf.

Golf Clubs

The maximum number of golf clubs a golfer may carry in his bag according to the rules is fourteen. Golf clubs are usually classified into two main groups: the woods and the irons. Most golf clubs on the market today have lightweight tempered-steel shafts with rubber grips. The length of the shaft and the loft of the club face are different for each club. In general, greater distance is gained with the longer and less lofted clubs. The shorter and more lofted clubs send the ball higher into the air and are used for lesser distances and greater accuracy. (See Figure 1.1.)

The Woods. A matched set of woods usually consists of numbers 1, 3, 4, and 5 (see Figure 1.2). The #1 club—the driver—has the longest shaft and its club face is almost vertical. Because of these factors it is the most difficult club to learn to hit with accuracy. It is used from the tee on holes where distance is essential. The #3 wood—the spoon—has greater loft and is used often on the fairway to hit a second shot. If a player does not have a #1 wood or if he/she is having difficulty

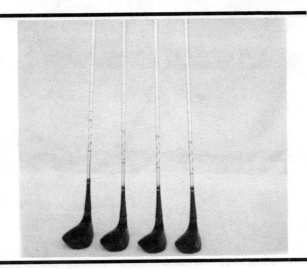

Figure 1.2 *The woods.*

with the #1, the #3 can be used from the tee. The loft of the clubs becomes greater as the numbers increase; therefore, the #4 and #5 woods have progressively greater lofts. Recommended woods for the beginning player are the #1 and #3 or the #1 and #4.

The Irons. The standard matched set of irons consists of clubs numbered 2 through 9 (see Figure 1.3), although sometimes the #2 is omitted and a wedge is added. The long irons, #2 and #3, are constructed for distance; the middle irons, #4, #5, and #6, are designed for higher trajectories. The short irons, #8 and #9, produce the highest loft and the least distance. As you get closer to the putting green, you will use increasingly higher-numbered clubs. Recommended irons for the beginning player are the #3, #5, #7, and #9 irons.

Some special irons, called wedges, are also available with many matched sets of clubs (see Figure 1.4). An all-purpose wedge has a wider sole than other irons, and it has a deep angle of loft and increased weight. It can be used for sand shots and for pitching to the green. More experienced golfers include a pitching wedge and a sand wedge in their set of clubs. The main difference

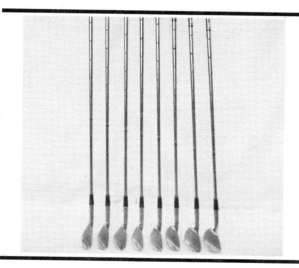

Figure 1.3 *The irons.*

in these two clubs is that the sand wedge has a more rounded sole, and the pitching wedge has a sharper and wider sole to aid in cutting a grassy surface.

The Putter. One of the most important and necessary clubs which all golfers must have is the putter; it is the most frequently used club in the set. There are hundreds of different styles, and selection of the type is a matter of individual preference. (See Figure 1.5.) The putter has almost no loft, and it is used to roll the ball along the ground either on or near the green.

Selection of Clubs

In selecting clubs it is wise for the beginner to consult a golf teacher or golf professional. There are differences in the length of a set of clubs, the swing weight of the clubs, and the flexibility of the shafts. The swing weight of the club refers to the distribution of weight of a club, and it is the proportion of the weight in the head of the club in comparison to the weight of the shaft and the grip. The swing weight is designated by the letters A, B, C, D, and F and by ten numerical gradations. Swing weights A and B are seldom used in standard clubs because they are very light. The average swing weight used by most women ranges between C-4 and C-7.

Figure 1.4 *The wedges.*

Stronger women and men golfers use clubs in the D-2 to D-6 range. The flexibility of the shaft, or the whip, of the club is usually designated by the letters X, S, R, A, and L, with X being a very stiff shaft and L being a whippy shaft. Most standard sets of women's clubs are in the R or S range. There is nothing on the club to indicate the swing weight and flexibility, but a golf professional or golf shop can check them for you.

Distance Expectancies

The distance you will attain with a particular club will

depend upon your ability and consistency. When you become a more experienced golfer you can expect a difference of between 10 to 20 yards between each of the woods and a distance of 10 yards between each of the irons. (See Figure 1.6.)

Other Equipment and Clothing

A golf bag and golf balls are next on the list of necessities for a golfer. A golf bag in which to carry your clubs can be small and simple or large and quite elaborate. If you are going to carry your clubs, a small bag is recommended; but if you are going to invest in a pull cart (or if you must use a motorized car), a larger

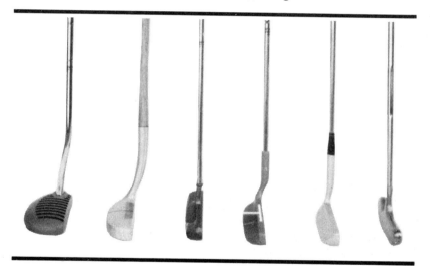

Figure 1.5 *Types of putters.*

bag can be purchased. Also on the market are types of bags and carts which are a combined arrangement and are light and easy to pull.

When buying golf balls you should know that there are three different compressions available, the highest of which is 100. Only the very powerful player uses 100 compression. A compression of 90 is used by a person who hits the ball quite long, and an 80-compression ball is used by the average golfer. It is well to understand that lesser compression does not indicate a lesser quality of the ball. For the beginning player there are cutproof balls with Surlyn covers which will last longer if shots are mis-hit. Along with balls you will need a supply of small wooden tees, which are used to tee up the ball at the beginning of each hole.

Golf shoes or shoes with short spikes on the soles and heels are not a necessity for a beginning golfer. However, if you can afford them they will prevent you from slipping on different types of grass and slopes as well as help you maintain your balance during your swing. If you do not wear golf shoes, be sure to wear a flat tennis shoe or a shoe of that type which will aid in balance and which will not mar the course or the putting green. A golf glove is also not essential, but if you find

	Woods		Irons			
	1	3	3	5	7	9
Women	180 yds. & up	165 yds & up	150	130	110	90
Men	200 yds & up	185 yds. & up	170	150	130	110

Figure 1.6 *Distance chart for the average golfer.*

Par	Women	Men
3	Up to 210 yds.	Up to 250 yds.
4	211 to 400 yds.	251 to 470 yds.
5	401 to 575 yds.	471 yds. & over
6	576 yds & over	

Figure 1.7 *Par computation.*

your hand slipping on the club, or if your skin blisters easily, it may be a good investment. For the right-handed golfer the left-hand glove is most often used, although some golfers wear gloves on both hands.

The clothing you wear on the golf course is dependent somewhat on your personal preference, but it should be comfortable so that it does not restrict or interfere with your swing. It should also be appropriate and in good taste. Most courses permit shorts or slacks for women and men, and many women and girls wear very attractive golf skirts. It is usually not permissible for men to play without a shirt, and short shorts and halters also are frowned upon as appropriate golf apparel.

THE GOLF COURSE

In learning the basics of the golf swing and the execution and use of various clubs, you might appreciate their importance and value more if you understand something about a golf course and how it is laid out. A full-length golf course has eighteen different holes ranging in size from 100 to 600 yards and covering a total area of from 100 to 150 acres. There are many courses which have nine holes, which are repeated to complete a full round, and there are other courses which have all short-distance holes. Each hole on the course is of a different length and configuration and includes a teeing ground, a fairway, the rough, obstructions, hazards (bunkers of sand or water hazards), a putting green, and a hole. There may not be hazards and obstructions on every hole, but some holes have an out-of-bounds area which is restricted to the golfer. Most holes also contain trees, which can present a problem if the golfer hits into them. Ideally, the player attempts to play the ball from the teeing area through the fairway and to the green, avoiding trees, the rough, and the hazards.

Each hole on the course has a "par" value, and each course has a total par, usually ranging from 70 to 72 for eighteen holes. Holes are assigned a par 3, 4, 5, or 6 according to their length. Par is the number of strokes assigned to a hole if a player were to play errorless golf. In the determination of par a player is allowed two putts on the green. The directions for computing par are shown in Figure 1.7. (These figures are taken from the United States Golf Association booklet, *Rules of Golf*.)

Some courses have all par-3 holes, and these types of courses are a good choice for beginners to use to get their first experiences on an actual course. They are also of value for players who wish to practice their short games or who do not have the time to play a long course. In addition, there are executive-type courses which have both par-3 and par-4 holes.

2

THE FULL SWING

LEARNING THE GOLF SWING

It is possible that some individuals with little or no instruction could develop a reasonably successful golf swing. However, because of the complex nature of the swing, most beginners will need some good instruction and visual guidelines if faulty swing habits are to be avoided.

Since the golf swing is relatively fast it should be thought of and felt as a whole movement. In the learning of motor skills most research points to the learning of "wholes" before "parts" when at all possible. The objective of the swing—which is to hit a ball to a target—should be uppermost in the golfer's mind. The swing itself should be taken over by the subconscious mind wherever possible so that the learner "lets it happen." It is recognized, however, that in the beginning stages the learner must consciously focus on some fundamental aspects of the swing. It is wise to keep these focal points simple and try not to think of more than one or two things at a time.

One of the most successful ways of learning a golf swing is for the learner to watch a demonstration of a good swing or to see a good visual aid and try to duplicate or imitate what was seen. Verbal and written

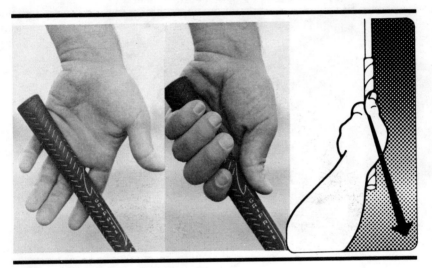

Figure 2.1 *The left-hand grip.*

instructions are also effective, and a combination of all three dimensions usually produces the best results.

Comments on Progression

Much of the literature on learning golf indicates that not everyone learns best with the same approach. Thus it is sometimes difficult to determine the best sequence for the beginning golfer to follow. Some seem to learn faster when they begin with short chip shots and progress to the full swing, and others do better when the process is reversed.

This book presents the basics of the full swing first, but for those who prefer another approach, the book need not be used in sequence.

BASIC ELEMENTS OF THE SWING

The elements that make up the golf swing are: (1) the grip, (2) stance and alignment, (3) the backswing, (4) the downswing, and (5) the follow-through. Combining these elements into a smooth, fluid, and consistent swing is the basic challenge for everyone who desires to play the game well.

The Grip

The grip has often been referred to as the most

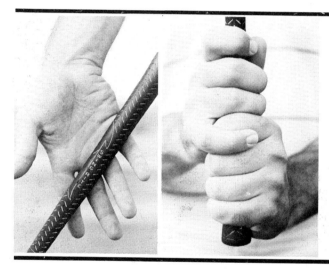

Figure 2.2   The right-hand grip.

important element of the golf swing. This is a slight overstatement, but its importance to the execution of good (consistent) golf shots cannot be minimized. A faulty grip is often the direct cause of poorly hit shots.

Among the good players there are slight variations of the grip, but all conform to a few proven fundamentals. The size of the hands, strength and flexibility of the body, and kind of body action used in striking the ball will all influence the type of grip best for each player.

The overlapping grip is clearly the most popular in the game today. Some fine players, however, such as

Jack Nicklaus, use the interlocking grip. Both are fundamentally sound in that they allow the hands to work together as a unit.

The Overlapping Grip. For the overlapping grip, position the club on the ground with the sole perfectly level and the face square to the target. Making sure that the back of the left hand* is also square to the target, press the shaft of the club up under the heel of the palm and directly across the top joint of the forefinger (see Figure 2.1). Close the fingers around the club and extend the thumb slightly to the right on the shaft. The V formed by the thumb and forefinger should point

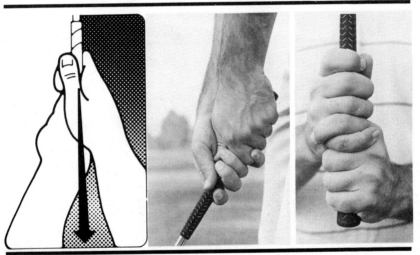

Figure 2.3 *The grip with both hands.* **Figure 2.4** *Interlocking grip.*

close to the direction of the right eye. To position the right hand on the club, face the palm toward the target and place the club so that the shaft lies across the top joint of all four fingers (see Figure 2.2). Slide the little finger up and over the forefinger of the left hand and lock it securely around it. Now simply fold the right hand over the top of the left thumb, with the right thumb gripping slightly to the left side of the club (see Figure 2.3). The V formed by the right thumb and

*In order to simplify the descriptions in this book, all hand and foot references are for right-handed golfers. Left-handers need to reverse these references and follow the same instructions.

forefinger should be pointing slightly right of the chin.

It is extremely important that the club not be held too tightly. "Squeezing" the club creates tension in the arms, which will prevent them from swinging freely and result in a loss of power. So a gentle firmness is best, with most of the pressure coming in the last three fingers of the left hand. Little or no pressure should be exerted in the right thumb and forefinger. Since it is a natural tendency for most golfers to unconsciously grip the club a little tighter on the downswing anyway, it is doubly important that the grip start out relaxed.

Figure 2.5 *Hands slightly ahead of clubface at address.*
Figure 2.6 *Side view of stance at position of address.*

The Interlocking Grip. The second type of grip, the interlocking, is identical to the overlapping, with one variation. The forefinger of the left hand comes off the club and "interlocks" with the little finger of the right hand (see Figure 2.4). Some arguments in favor of this grip are that it is more natural and easier to learn, and that it locks the hands together more securely. The strongest argument against it seems to be that there is a feeling of having less control by taking the left finger off the club. In the beginning, either grip you use will most likely feel unnatural, so it is recommended that you experiment with both until you find which works best for you or which feels the most comfortable.

Technique Check Points

1. Back of left hand and palm of right hand face toward target.

2. V's of both hands point slightly right of chin.

3. Little finger of right hand overlaps or interlocks with forefinger of left hand.

4. Light grip with most of pressure coming in last three fingers of left hand.

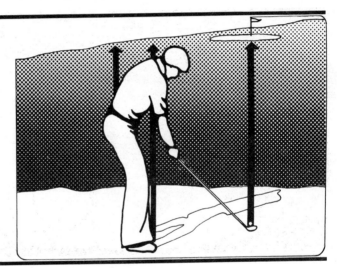

Figure 2.7 *Body aligned left but parallel to target line.*

Stance and Alignment

The stance involves the relationship of the feet to the ball, weight distribution, and the posture and alignment of the body. If your clubface and body are not aligned correctly to the target, or your posture is poor, some compensating moves in your swing will be required. This usually involves overworking your hands and shoulders, which will destroy any chance for a smooth, rhythmical swing.

A good way to begin the setup is to establish in your mind the desired line of flight to the target. Next, with the left hand, set the clubface behind the ball so that it is square to the target, extending the left arm firmly so that a straight line is formed from the shoulder to the ball. As the right hand is added, the hands should be in the desired position—slightly ahead of the clubface (see Figure 2.5). The right elbow should be relaxed. The knees are slightly flexed with the weight a little more toward the balls of the feet. Bend over from the hips so as to allow the arms to hang down naturally (see Figure 2.6). The feet, knees, hips, and shoulders should be on a line parallel to the target line. A misconception held by many golfers is that the body should be aimed at the target. In reality, the body must be lined up left of the

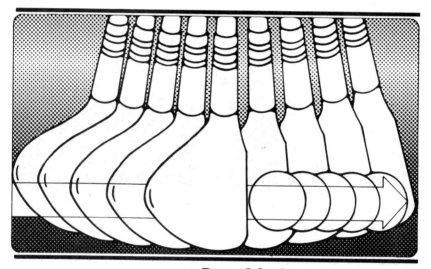

Figure 2.8 Correct clubhead path.

target but parallel to the target line (see Figure 2.7).

To hit straight golf shots, the ideal path for the clubhead is to approach the ball from inside the target line to along the line at impact. After impact, the club-head should continue toward the target momentarily before it swings naturally back to the inside (see Figure 2.8).

The width of the feet in the stance varies with the club being used. For the woods and long irons, the feet should be approximately shoulder width. The stance narrows with the shorter clubs. The best spot to position the ball in relation to the feet is where the clubhead will make contact just before it starts moving upward. For most players this is somewhere between the inner left heel and the center of the stance. It is recommended, however, that you position the ball opposite the inner left heel on all full shots and simply move your right foot closer to the ball when hitting the shorter clubs (see Figure 2.9). Keep your weight slightly to the right side with your head positioned back of an imaginary line drawn from the ball (see Figure 2.10).

The importance of a setup that produces correct alignment and posture cannot be emphasized enough. A faulty setup will almost always force the golfer into swing errors that will result in poorly hit shots.

Figure 2.9 *Width of stance.*   Figure 2.10 *Head behind ball.*

Technique Check Points

1. Clubhead square to target.

2. Feet approximately shoulder width for longer clubs, and narrowed accordingly for shorter clubs.

3. Weight slightly toward balls of the feet and a little to right side.

4. Feet, knees, hips, and shoulders parallel to target line.

5. Head slightly back of ball.

6. Clubhead path is from inside target line, to along target line, and back inside.

The Backswing

It is extremely difficult to get good rhythm in the swing starting from a static position. Most of the good players utilize either a "waggle" or a "forward press" (some use both) just before taking the club back. The waggle is a relaxed moving of the club back and forth behind the ball (see Figure 2.11). There is no shoulder turn; just the hands and arms move. In the forward

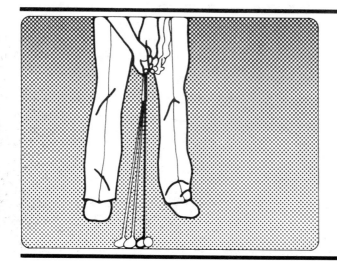

Figure 2.11 *The waggle.*

press, the knees make a slight move toward the target, or there is a delicate forward press of the hands and arms. Some form of either the waggle or forward press is almost essential in order to accomplish a smooth, coordinated swing through the ball.

The backswing is initiated by the nearly simultaneous movement of the hands, arms, and shoulders (actually, the hands move slightly ahead of the arms, which in turn lead the shoulders). Without breaking the wrists, slowly move the club straight back from the ball, keeping the clubhead low to the ground.

Maintain the club on this path for about as far back as the right foot, where the turning of the shoulders and hips will bring the club naturally to the inside as it moves to the top of the backswing (see Figure 2.12). The left arm remains firm but not rigid, while the right elbow bends just as the club begins its inside path to the top.

At the top of the backswing, the ideal is to have the fullest shoulder turn and highest arm swing possible. This will provide for maximum clubhead acceleration through the ball with the least amount of effort. A partial shoulder turn and arm swing will cause most players to try to "muscle" the ball with their arms and shoulders, resulting in a variety of bad shots.

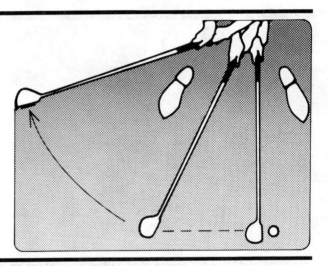

Figure 2.12 *Backswing club path.*

Somewhere between the takeaway and the top of the backswing, the wrists need to "cock" so that added power can be attained upon their release in the hitting area. To do this correctly, the left wrist hinges at the base of the thumb, keeping the back of the left hand in a straight line relationship with the arm (see Figure 2.13). This action will automatically fold the back of the right wrist inward.

Nicklaus and other fine players feel that this cocking of the wrists should occur naturally near the top of the backswing. In the past few years, however, a number of other touring professionals have begun to cock the wrists as early as possible in the backswing (see Figure 2.14). The advantage of this earlier cocking of the wrists is: (1) a smoother transition from the backswing to the downswing and (2) the left arm can more naturally control the downswing with a pull rather than a right-arm push. Both techniques have proven to be successful, but if you are just learning the game, setting the angle earlier in the backswing is recommended.

Legs. As the hips turn to follow the shoulders, the left knee remains flexed and moves inward toward the right knee. The right knee should also be kept slightly flexed, with the weight remaining on the inside of the

Figure 2.13   Wrist cock.

right foot throughout the backswing (see Figure 2.15).

Head. The chin should be set a little to the right, giving the left shoulder room to make a full turn. Trying to hold the head too steady or rigid can restrict a full armswing, but keep the movement to a minimum.

Technique Check Points

1. Wrists firm on takeaway.

2. Start club out straight back and low to ground.

3. Left arm firm.

4. Cock the wrists early.

5. Full shoulder turn at top.

6. Knees remain flexed.

7. Chin tilts slightly to right.

8. Weight on inside of right foot.

9. Keep it slow.

The Downswing

In order to achieve a smooth transition from the backswing to the downswing, the position at the top can only be held for an instant. In fact, the knees should be

Figure 2.14 *(a) Early wrist cock. (b) Late wrist cock.*

moving laterally back toward the target before the arms and shoulders fully complete the backswing. Thus the knees begin the downswing, followed by a releasing of the hips, shoulders, and arms. As in the backswing, these movements must be smoothly coordinated into a nearly simultaneous action. So, in effect, the swing is not made up of a series of separate motions, but should be thought of as a flowing, uninterrupted action from the position of address all the way through the finish of the swing. The left side and arm should be in total control of the downswing. As the knees drive toward the target, the weight is transferred from the inside of the right foot to the left foot before impact (see Figure 2.16).

As mentioned earlier, it is virtually impossible to keep the head absolutely still and make a comfortable swing at the ball. However, it is vitally important that the head remain behind the ball at impact. Allowing the head to move forward toward the target during the downswing will result in a loss of power and create an inconsistent hitting pattern as well.

The Follow-Through

After impact, the hips and shoulders turn, facing

Figure 2.15 *Knee position and weight distribution in backswing.*

the target, and the arms finish high. Notice that at the top of the follow-through, the right heel is off the ground and pivoted almost parallel to the target line (see Figure 2.17).

An important reminder is to stay down and through the ball long enough in the hitting area. This means more than not lifting the head too soon; it means keeping the knees flexed all the way to the top of the follow-through. The upper body will raise somewhat well after the ball has been hit, but the knees should never come to full extension.

TEMPO

Correct application of all the aforementioned mechanics of the golf swing can still result in inconsistent and poorly hit golf shots if proper timing is missing. All good players have developed a consistent tempo or rhythm to their swings. Some swing much faster than others, but all have an element of smoothness incorporated in their own natural tempo. Most high-handicap players swing too fast to allow the proper

Figure 2.16 *The downswing.*

sequence of the swing to happen. On the other hand, it is possible to swing too slowly and deliberately, with the result that a full unleashing of power never occurs. Each player must develop a tempo that is natural, the important elements being smoothness and consistency.

Technique Check Points

1. Knees initiate downswing.

2. Left side and arm in control.

Figure 2.17 *The follow-through.*

3. Weight transfers to left foot before impact.

4. Head behind ball at impact.

5. Knees remain flexed through shot.

6. Body facing target on follow-through.

7. Keep swing smooth and natural.

COMPARING THE WOODS AND IRONS

Essentially, the swing fundamentals are the same for the woods as the irons. The most significant difference is in the arc of the swing, or the swing plane. Because the

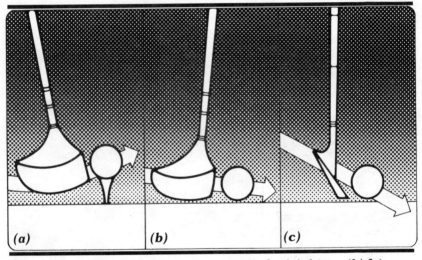

Figure 2.18 *Angle of club on downswing for (a) driver, (b) fairway wood, and (c) iron.*

woods are longer clubs, the swing into the ball will be a little flatter than with the irons. This should be a natural consequence of the longer club, however, and not a conscious effort on the part of the golfer to alter the swing plane.

The Tee Shot

When the ball is elevated on a wooden tee, the flatter swing plane is more pronounced. The feeling should be one of "sweeping" the ball off the tee. Oftentimes the inexperienced golfer will tee the ball up too low, especially when using the driver. This will almost always produce a shot with a low trajectory (and loss of distance) because the ball will be contacted only on the lower half of the clubface. A good rule to follow when teeing up a ball is to set it high enough so that approximately half the ball is above the top of the clubhead as it rests on the ground.

Fairway Woods

When using a wood for a fairway shot (usually the #3 or #4 wood) your swing plane has to be more like that of the irons—down and through the ball. The greatest difficulty the average player has with the fairway wood shot is getting the ball airborne. By swinging down and through the ball so that the sole of the club makes "light" contact with the ground just as the ball is being struck, the natural pitch of the clubface will direct the ball upward. Be careful not to make the angle of the downswing too severe. The grass in front of the ball should appear as if it had just been mowed. If the club digs up the turf or takes a divot, as with the irons, the swing plane is too steep (see Figure 2.18).

Short Irons

When hitting a full #7, #8, or #9 (wedge), the most important factor is accuracy rather than distance. Too many golfers are in the habit of using a club that requires maximum effort to reach the green, and end up either pulling or pushing the shot badly off line or mis-hitting it altogether. So be sure to use enough club to allow for a smooth, unforced swing.

Your feet should be closer together with the short irons, and slightly open. Because of the shorter length of the irons, the swing is more upright; the shorter the iron, the more upright the swing. The ball should be contacted on the downswing, and if it has been hit correctly there should be a small divot taken in front of it. If there is no divot, you are not hitting down through the ball sufficiently, and it won't attain the desired trajectory or holding action (backspin) on the green.

Middle Irons

When using the middle irons, square your stance and widen it some for better balance. Since these irons are longer in length, the swing plane will be a little flatter than with the short irons. Otherwise, the swing fundamentals are the same.

Long Irons

The difference between the technique necessary for the long irons in relation to the other irons is negligible. Yet the long irons have proven to be much more difficult for most players. Because of the straighter face of the long iron, the tendency is to try and lift or scoop the ball

Figure 2.19 *Eight-frame series of full swing.*

to get it airborne. The usual result is a variety of mis-hit shots.

Assume a shoulder-width stance and contact the ball with a little less "down and through" action than with the shorter irons. If the ball has been hit correctly, there will be less of a divot taken than with the short irons.

You will enjoy much greater success with the long irons if you will maintain the same swing tempo with them as with the short irons. Overswinging is one of the most common factors in the poor execution of the long irons.

As you can see, the technique is very similar for all the irons, the main difference being the arc of the swing. Developing a feel for just the right degree of swing plane that will bring the clubhead down and through the ball cleanly and with consistency is one of the fundamental challenges of the game. It naturally requires practice, but the rewards will more than justify it.

THE SHORT GAME

To score well consistently requires the successful execution of the shots that make up the short game, i.e. pitching, chipping, and putting. Having the ability to drive the ball a long distance is a distinct advantage, particularly when it is done accurately. But a good touch around the greens can more than offset the disadvantage of not being able to hit long.

PITCHING

A pitch shot is hit with a high-ball trajectory and relatively little roll when it lands on the green. This type of shot is required when there are bunkers (sand traps) or hilly terrain between the ball and the flag stick (see Figure 3.1). The #9 iron, or wedge, is the club normally used to execute this delicate shot.

The feet should be a little closer together than with a full 9-iron shot and slightly more open (left foot back from the target line). Make sure your shoulders remain parallel to the target line or your shots will most likely be pulled left of where you are looking (see Figure 3.2). When a lot of backspin is desired, keep your weight to the left side throughout the swing, which allows you to hit the ball more on the downswing. The clubface should be opened and the hands ahead of the ball at address.

There is a common tendency with the pitch shot to take too large a backswing, followed by a slowing down of the forward swing and little or no follow-through. Just the reverse is a more correct sequence. Only the amount of backswing should be taken to allow a firm accelerated hit through the ball and proper follow-through. Practicing this shot at different distances is the only way to develop a feel for the proper combination of backswing, forward swing, and follow-through.

Technique Check Points

1. Feet slightly open and closer together than with a full 9-iron shot.

2. Keep shoulders parallel to target line.

3. Shorten backswing and accelerate through the ball.

4. Head is steady until after ball is hit.

CHIPPING

When the ball is closer to the green (5 to 10 yards) and there are no traps or hilly terrain on line to the cup, a "pitch and run" or "chip" shot is usually the safest and easiest shot to get close to the hole (Figure 3.1). This shot is hit lower to the ground, with rolling action on the ball. The idea is to land the ball just on the putting surface and allow for maximum roll on the green.

A club with less loft, such as a #6 or #7 iron, is usually used for these shots. However, many excellent "chippers" use a more lofted club and lay the clubface forward so as to provide a bigger and broader hitting surface. Some players use a different club for different situations, such as distance from the green and the amount of roll desired. Others use the same club for almost all situations, with the idea that a more consistent feel can be developed. There is merit to both approaches, and only through experimenting will you be able to determine what works best for you.

Just enough movement of the knees and hips should be allowed to make a free, comfortable swing through the ball. The ball should be struck with a descending blow, keeping the left wrist firm to avoid a "scooping" action (see Figure 3.3). Floppy wrists will

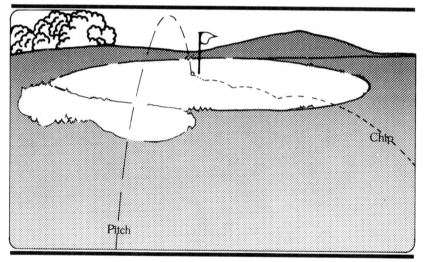

Figure 3.1 *Short-approach shots.*

make it virtually impossible to develop any degree of consistency with your chip shots. By keeping the wrists firm, the ball will react the same way all the time. You won't find yourself hitting halfway to the hole one time and ten feet past the next. The direction of the shot will be on line more consistently as well.

Special effort should be expended early to develop this part of your game. Being able to get down in two from the edge of the green is a great stroke saver, and often keeps your scores comparable to players with a longer game.

Technique Check Points

1. Grip down on club an inch or two and move closer to the ball.

2. Slightly open stance.

3. Only slight movement of the knees and hips.

4. Firm left wrist.

5. Strike ball with a descending blow.

6. Keep head steady until after ball is hit.

Figure 3.2 *Open stance, shoulders parallel to target line.*

PUTTING

One of the more distressing experiences in golf is to cover 400 or more yards to the green in only two shots, and wind up taking three or four more strokes with the putter to hole the ball from 30 feet or less. Yet this is not at all uncommon, even with more experienced players. It's an indication of just how important this part of the game is.

On a par-72 course, 36 shots are allotted to reach the greens and 36 for putts. So, in a real sense, it can be said that putting is half the game of golf. Fortunately, because the stroke is the shortest and simplest to execute, almost everyone can attain some degree of accuracy after a short term of practice.

Putting lends itself to individual style and technique more than any other aspect of the game. In fact, there are nearly as many different putting styles as there are golfers. Even among the professionals it wouldn't be difficult to pick out some variation in almost every player. A short period of experimentation should help you settle on a style that will work for you. The main thing is to find a grip and stance that feels comfortable and natural.

The choice of club varies a great deal. Here again

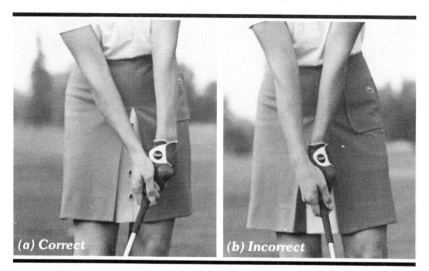

(a) Correct   (b) Incorrect

Figure 3.3   Firm left wrist.

it's a matter of selecting a putter that you like to swing, one that appeals to you and gives you confidence.

The following fundamentals relating to the putting stroke will serve as a guide in establishing a sound putting style of your own.

The Grip

Most good putters use the "reverse overlap" grip where the forefinger of the left hand comes off the club and overlaps the fingers of the right hand, as in Figure 3.4. The putting grip also differs from the normal grip in that the left hand is turned more to the left and the right hand more to the right. The inside of the left thumb will be resting against the shaft, while the right thumb should extend straight down the shaft. The wrists should be slightly arched as in Figure 3.5.

Hold the club lightly, with most of the pressure in the last three fingers of the left hand. By following these grip fundamentals the hand rotation will be more inhibited during the stroke, enabling the putterface to remain square to the target longer. The restricted wrist action also makes the putt more of an arm-and-shoulder movement. This decreases the margin of error for mis-hitting the putt, which is more likely to occur when the stroke is too "wristy."

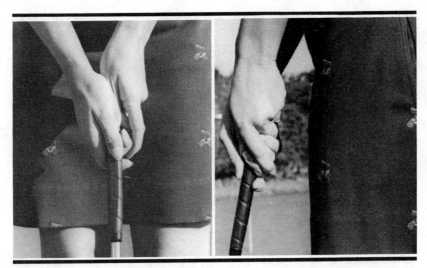

Figure 3.4 *Reverse overlap grip.*   **Figure 3.5** *Wrists arched.*

The Stance

The knees should be slightly flexed and the weight centered between the balls and heels of the feet. The hips should be bent so that the eyes are directly over the target line (see Figure 3.6). The amount of bend in the hips will be influenced by the distance the ball is positioned from the feet. The closer the ball, the more erect will be the stance, and the farther you stand from the ball, the greater the bend in the body. Most players can maintain a better visual line to the hole if they stand a little more erect, so it is recommended that the ball be played no more than four or five inches out from the toes, and somewhere between the center of your stance to inside your left heel.

Bob Toski, one of the more respected teaching professionals in the game today, feels that the weight should be slightly to the right side so that you have the feeling of staying behind the ball and stroking more toward the hole. Whether your feet are positioned in a square, open, or closed stance is strictly a matter of personal preference. Whatever stance allows you to stroke the ball with the greatest amount of confidence and accuracy should be used. Some good putters set

Figure 3.6 *Putting stance.*   **Figure 3.7 *Putting stroke.***

their elbows out away from their bodies, but keeping them in closer to your sides will give you a more compact and consistent stroke action with less margin for error.

The Stroke

The putting stroke is made primarily with the arms, the left hand and arm being in control. Breaking the wrists on the backswing, particularly on long putts, is unavoidable, but the left wrist should be kept firm on the forward swing. It is generally agreed that the putterhead should be taken back as low as possible and that it should finish low. This can happen only if the left wrist and arm are allowed to move forward as the ball is struck (Figure 3.7).

Some good putters take the putterhead inside the target line on the backswing and back to the inside on the follow-through. Others favor keeping the putterhead along the target line throughout the entire stroke. Either technique is sound. The important thing is that the putterhead is square to the desired line at impact.

Too conscious an effort to keep your body still during the putt will often destroy your relaxation. A little freedom of movement is all right as long as your head doesn't move forward before you strike the ball.

One of the more common problems with the putting stroke is taking too long a backswing and then decelerating the club just before impact. The ball rolls truer toward the hole when a short backswing is taken and there is a slight acceleration of the putterhead through the ball. The length of the follow-through should generally match the length of the backswing.

With long putts it is better to concentrate on distance, whereas with short putts accuracy should be the focal point. Since so many putts come up short, you need to be conscious of stroking firmly enough to get the ball up to the hole.

Reading the Greens

Aside from your own stroke, there are a number of other factors that influence the roll of the ball on the green. Conditions that will make the ball roll slower are: (1) grass that is damp or feels soft under foot, (2) greens on which the grass hasn't been cut recently, (3) putting against the grain of the grass, and (4) an uphill putt to the hole. Reversing these conditions will naturally cause the ball to roll faster than normal.

The art of judging the line and speed of putts, particularly those on slopes, can only be developed with practice. A suggestion for the sidehill putts is to keep the ball above the hole so that it will always be falling toward the cup. If the putt doesn't drop and you have hit it with the right speed, it will at least finish near the hole.

Technique Check Points

1. Both hands turned a little outward; wrists slightly arched.

2. Reverse overlap grip (forefinger of left hand overlaps fingers of right hand).

3. Knees flexed with weight slightly to the right side.

4. Eyes are directly over target line.

5. Ball positioned four or five inches out from toes, between center of stance to inside of left heel.

6. Elbows comfortably close to sides.

7. Left wrist firm in forward swing.

8. Putterhead low throughout swing.

9. Head steady until after the ball has been hit.

10. Short backswing, accelerate through putt.

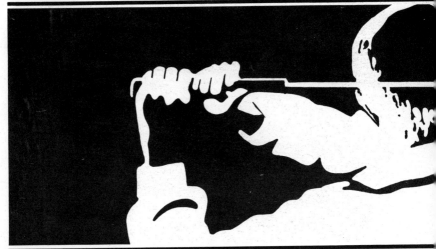

THE TROUBLE SHOTS

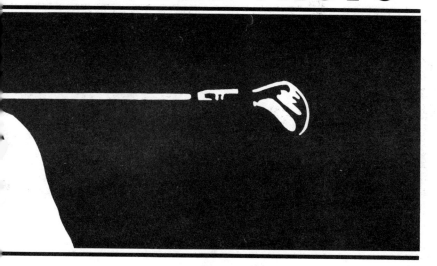

I t is rare when even the best players are able to play a round of golf without having to make a shot from the rough, a sand trap, or an uneven lie. Most golf courses are designed to provide at least one of these challenges on every hole. Having the knowledge and skill to successfully execute these shots will not only bring your scores down but will bolster your confidence as a player and provide greater enjoyment from the game.

HITTING OUT OF THE ROUGH

One of the more common tendencies of the average golfer is to try to get too much distance when hitting from the rough. More often than not, the wrong club is used and the result is an additional stroke or two just to get the ball to the fairway. Better strategy would be to sacrifice distance and play your first shot safely onto the fairway. Barring any further mishaps, you can still make bogey and with a little luck, you could even save par.

For long shots out of tall grass that isn't too thick, a #3 or #4 wood will produce better results than a long or medium iron. This is due to the large, flat head and tapered hosel of the wood, allowing it to cut through the grass with less resistance. However, until you have had sufficient time to practice this shot, using a short iron to the fairway is still a wiser choice.

Figure 4.1 *Hitting out of thick grass.*

For shorter shots from the tall rough, use the club that has the most loft and will still carry the ball to the green. The height and thickness of the grass will be a definite factor in your club selection. With deeper grass, you will need a more lofted club, even at the risk of not getting the ball the desired distance. Shots hit from the rough won't hold the green as well as those hit from the fairway, because of the grass buildup between the clubhead and the ball, so figure to play the ball shorter and allow for more roll.

When addressing a ball in tall grass, place the clubhead an inch or so above and behind the ball to avoid the possibility of catching it in the grass on the takeaway. The club must be taken up and brought back on a steeper angle to reduce the amount of grass between the clubface and the ball. Also, the club should be held a little firmer than normal to prevent it from turning. Open the clubface slightly and, in thick grass, direct your swing an inch or two behind the ball so that the force of the club will dislodge it instead of actually contacting the ball itself (see Figure 4.1). Keep your head still and be sure to have the club accelerating in the hitting area.

The short rough should pose little problem because most shots can be played normally. The problem is more mental, since you don't have a nice "fluffy" lie in the center of the fairway. Just be sure to make a firm stroke down and through the ball with whatever club you use.

Technique Check Points

1. Address ball an inch or two above the turf.

2. Hold club a little firmer.

3. Takeaway and downswing are at steeper angle.

4. Open clubface slightly.

5. When grass is thick contact turf an inch or two behind the ball.

6. Accelerate club in hitting area.

SAND PLAY

It is interesting to note that the professionals think the sand shot is the easiest shot in golf, while just the opposite is true for the nonprofessional. The big difference, of course, is that the tour players have a clear idea of what it is they want to do and have spent many hours in the sand acquiring the necessary skills to do it consistently.

When hitting from a sand trap near the green and only a short pitch shot is required, a #9 iron — or preferably a sand wedge — is the club to use. The sand wedge is heavier and has a flange which allows it to glide through the sand with greater ease than the #9 iron. Occasionally your ball will be positioned in a trap so as to allow you to use your putter, but most of the time a type of "explosion" shot will be required. To execute this shot, open your stance and settle your feet in the sand to give you a firm base. Keep your weight slightly to the left side and play the ball off the instep of the left foot. Use your normal grip and shorten it up for better control. The clubhead should be laid back but not open. This will put your left wrist in a slightly concave position (see Figure 4.2). Remember, the rules don't allow your clubhead to touch the sand before the downswing.

(a) Correct   *(b) Incorrect*

Figure 4.2 *Explosion shot from sand trap.*

With the clubface square to the target, take the club straight back from the ball. Your swing should be a little more upright and should be allowed to come inside the line somewhat. Bring the clubhead down so that it strikes the sand three or four inches behind the ball (closer to two inches if using a #9 iron). The flange, not the leading edge, should make contact with the sand first (see Figure 4.3).

As the club cuts under the ball, the sand will send the ball upward and land it softly on the green. The left hand and arm again control the shot, and the left wrist should not be allowed to collapse. Be sure to follow through and not leave the club buried in the sand. As with all golf shots, your head must remain steady until the ball has been hit.

The texture of the sand and the degree to which the ball is resting down in it will determine the angle of the clubface and how deep a cut to make in the sand (see Figure 4.4). The club will not penetrate as deeply in coarse or wet sand as it does when it is finer.

It will take practice to gain confidence in playing the sand shot, but for those who will take the time it can become one of the easiest to perform because there is a wider margin for error.

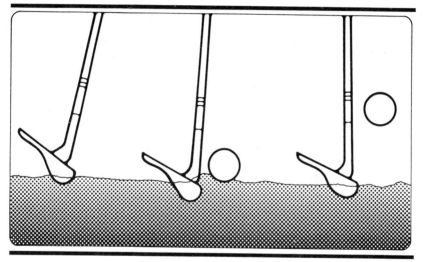

Figure 4.3 *Contact sand with flange.*

Technique Check Points

1. Open stance and settle feet in sand.

2. Ball positioned off instep of left foot and weight on left side.

3. Shorten grip and lay clubhead back square behind ball.

4. Use more upright swing.

5. Clubhead contacts sand 3 or 4 inches behind ball.

6. Keep left wrist firm and follow-through.

7. Keep head steady.

FAIRWAY TRAPS

When faced with a long shot from a fairway trap, any iron or even a #3, #4, or #5 wood can be used. Because your pivot is slightly restricted on these sand shots, you should use one more club (one that will give you greater distance) than you would normally use. Otherwise, play the shot as a regular shot, making certain that the clubhead contacts the ball before it enters the sand.

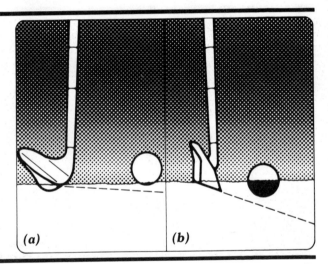

Figure 4.4 *(a) Club angle when ball is sitting up; (b) ball partially buried.*

UNEVEN LIES

Along with the challenge of tall grass and sand traps, you will also be faced with four different types of uneven lies — uphill, downhill, and sidehill where the ball is either above or below your feet. With a little understanding and some minor compensations, these shots need not be a problem.

Uphill Lie

When you hit a shot from an uphill lie, the ball will fly higher than usual because the slope of the ground tends to increase the loft of the club. Also, because your balance is not as stable, a shorter grip and less backswing is recommended. Thus it is usually a good idea to use one club stronger than you normally would.

Your weight should be on your right foot and the ball positioned opposite your left heel. Aim a little right, since this setup usually produces a right-to-left action, leaving your ball left of the target (see Figure 4.5).

Downhill Lie

The downhill lie is a more difficult shot for most players. As opposed to the uphill lie, the ball tends to

Figure 4.5   Uphill lie.   **Figure 4.6   Downhill lie.**

stay low and usually drifts right of the target. A more lofted club is recommended, along with a shorter swing for better control. Also, using a more upright swing and being particularly aware of staying down all the way through the shot will be a big help in getting the ball up from this lie.

Since your clubhead will reach the ground sooner from the downhill lie, position the ball a little farther back in your stance. Play to the right of your target to counter the anticipated fade or slice to the right (see Figure 4.6).

Sidehill—Ball Above Feet

This shot should be played much like the uphill lie. The most significant difference is the tendency to fall away from the shot during the swing. To counter this, keep your weight more forward on the balls of your feet.

Since the ball is closer to you in this lie, shorten your grip so your arms can remain fully extended, as in a normal shot. A shorter swing will also produce cleaner hits more consistently. Again, play your shot right of the target to allow for the hook, or pull action, that normally occurs from this lie (see Figure 4.7).

Figure 4.7 *Sidehill—ball above feet.*

Sidehill—Ball Below Feet

This lie seems to be the most difficult for most players due to the awkward position of address and the much tougher challenge of staying down throughout the swing.

To guard against falling forward on this shot, flex your knees a little more and keep your weight toward your heels. Stand a little closer to the ball and use one club stronger to allow a shorter swing for better control. The ball usually fades to the right as in the downhill lie, so play a little left to compensate for it (see Figure 4.8).

Figure 4.8 Sidehill—ball below feet.

INFORMATION FOR PLAYING THE GAME

In this chapter you will be introduced to some of the information which is necessary before you try out your golf skills on a golf course. No matter what your ability, you should be knowledgeable about the etiquette, safety, scoring, types of play, handicapping, and basic rules of the game.

ETIQUETTE

The etiquette of golf is based upon courtesy to other golfers, fast and safe play, and respect and proper care of the course. The following suggestions should be followed:

Courtesy to Other Golfers

1. Regardless of their ability, be courteous to all golfers.

2. Stand quietly, motionless, and out of the direct line of others as they hit. Talking and distractions can be disturbing. Do not allow your shadow to interfere with anyone's line of play.

3. Be sure to identify the ball you are playing. If it is the same make and number as that of another player in your group, make a mark on it so that you do not play the wrong ball.

4. Try not to step on the putting line of other players on the green. Mark and lift your ball when you are requested to do so by another player. Place a coin or a marker behind your ball. If your ball interferes with another player's putting line, use your putter head to measure one or more lengths to the side of your ball's position.

5. If you are attending the flagstick for another player, stand to the side of the hole and hold the pennant and the flagstick. The player who is closest to the hole usually attends the flagstick.

6. Compliment others on good strokes, but avoid negative comments if they have bad strokes.

Playing Without Delay

1. Be ready to play when it is your turn. Avoid delays caused by taking numerous practice swings. Walk rapidly between shots.

2. Let faster groups go through. Signal them to go ahead and wait until they are out of range before you hit. On a busy golf course there should not be an open hole ahead of you.

3. Leave bags and carts off the green and to the side which is nearest the next tee.

4. Leave the green immediately when you have finished the hole. Mark your scores as you are moving to the next hole or as you are waiting to tee off.

5. Watch your ball carefully at all times. Spot its position with a tree or some object on the course.

6. Help another player in your group find a ball which is possibly lost. Also help another player determine if a ball is out of bounds. Wave through the group behind you if you are delaying play. To save time be sure to play a provisional ball if you think you might be out of bounds or lost.

7. If you are a beginner and you get into a situation in which you are taking a number of strokes without much result, such as can happen in the rough, pick up your ball and place it where you can hit it. Keeping accurate score at this level of play is less important than keeping pace.

Safety on the Course

1. Stand a safe distance away from a player hitting a ball or taking a practice swing.

2. Do not hit your shot until the golfers ahead of you are well out of range. Do not underestimate your ability.

3. If your ball goes in the direction of other golfers, shout "fore" to warn them.

4. Drive carefully and courteously if you are using an electric car.

5. Avoid playing golf during a lightning storm. Precautions for your safety in such an event are found in the USGA rules.

Proper Care of the Golf Course

1. Replace all divots (loose turf). Leave the golf course in the same or better shape than you found it.

2. Repair ball marks on the green. Lift up the grass with a tee, then press it down firmly.

3. Do not drop the flagstick on the green. Lay it down carefully. Also avoid dropping clubs on the putting green.

4. Avoid scuffing your feet or making marks on the putting green. Walk carefully.

5. After you have hit from a bunker (sand trap), use a club or rake to smooth out club marks and footprints. Enter and leave the bunker at the point nearest the ball or where it is low.

SCORING AND THE SCORECARD

Scoring in golf is fairly simple. You count the number of strokes you take on each hole. At the end of the round your final score is the sum of these strokes. If you completely miss the ball, this counts as a stroke. Penalty strokes, which will be explained later in the section on rules, also count in the computation of your score. A sample scorecard is shown in Figure 5.1. There

Champion Tees-Blue 70.1	389	535	150	332	320	382	203	541	395	3247
Regular Tees-White 68.2	368	510	146	325	298	362	186	521	376	3092
Men's Par	4	5	3	4	4	4	3	5	4	36
Handicap Strokes	8	7	17	13	15	5	11	3		
Hole	1	2	3	4	5	6	7	8	9	OUT
Women's Par	4	5	3	4	4	4	3	5	4	36
Women's Tees-Red 72.1	355	492	138	316	286	351	141	498	357	2934
Handicap Strokes	8	3	15	11	13	7	17	1	9	12

DATE _____   SCORER _____

Figure 5.1 *Sample scorecard.*

are many minor differences in scorecards, but the following information is generally contained on the card. A description of each item follows:

Hole Numbers. On this card they are shown through the center of the card.

Players' Names and Scores. Names are entered in the wide spaces on the left of the card, and the scores on each hole—along with the 9 and 18 hole totals—are entered on the small spaces.

Champion Tees (blue). The yardages used by

professional golfers and low-handicap amateurs. These are not included on all courses.

Regular Tees (white). The yardages used by men players.

Women's Tees (red). The yardages used by women players.

Par. On this course, par is the same for women and men although the yardages are different. On some courses par varies by one or two strokes.

Course Ratings. The difficulty ratings which have been established by a committee according to standards set up by USGA. These numerical ratings are listed

375	138	421	376	516	211	413	405	526	3381	6628		
347	129	405	352	496	171	403	376	503	3182	6274		
4	3	4	4	5	3	4	4	5	36	72		
14	18	1	16	2	10	4	12	6		TOTAL	HDCP	NET
10	11	12	13	14	15	16	17	18	IN			
4	3	4	4	5	3	4	4	5	36	72		
326	114	354	326	487	142	345	346	468	2908	5842		
18	5	14	2	16	4	10	6					

ATTESTED BY _____

after each set of tees.

Handicap Strokes. These figures indicate the ranking of the holes for women and men on which handicap strokes will be given. Handicapping is further explained in a later section in this chapter.

Scorer. In competition, a player's score is recorded by another player.

Attested By. The player checks the accuracy of his or her score before signing the scorecard.

Yardages. All yardage is measured from the center of each teeing area to the center of the green.

TYPES OF PLAY OR COMPETITION

There are two major categories of competition: stroke play and match play.

Stroke Play

The objective of stroke play is to shoot the lowest possible total score for whatever number of rounds is designated for the tournament. Usually a professional tournament consists of 72 holes or four rounds, but many club, school, and collegiate tournaments consist of 18, 36, or 54 holes. If a tie occurs in stroke play there may be an 18 hole playoff, a "sudden-death" playoff, or whatever is stipulated by the tournament rules.

Match Play

The objective of match play is to shoot a lower score than your opponent on each hole. The player who wins the most holes wins the match, and the winner may be decided before the last hole. If a player is 4 up on an opponent with only 3 holes to play, the match is completed (4–3). If the match is tied at the end of 18 holes, the players continue to play until one of them wins a hole. Match-play tournaments are usually elimination types of contests, with the competition continuing until just one player remains.

Besides competing as an individual against other individuals, there are other ways to compete as you play. Often one two-player team will play another two-player team in either stroke play or match play. Each team member plays his or her own ball, but only the lowest score will count as the team's score on a particular hole. When handicaps (see next section) are used, the team's score on a hole is the lowest net score shot by an individual player.

HANDICAPPING

A method to make it possible for golfers of unequal playing abilities to play on more even terms is called handicapping. A golfer's handicap is computed on the basis of the scores which are shot combined with the difficulty of the course played. For example, if a player shot 94 and the course rating is 70.1, the handicap differential would be 23.9. The last 20 handicap differentials are considered, and the 10 lowest of these are averaged to arrive at the average differential. Then 96 percent of the average differential (when rounded off to the closest whole number) becomes the handicap. If the average differential on your 10 best rounds is 22.8, then your handicap is 21.8, or 22 when rounded off.

When a golfer with a handicap of 22 competes with a golfer with a 12 handicap, 10 strokes will be given to the other player. The 22 handicapper will get one stroke on each of 10 holes. These will be taken from the holes on the scorecard ranked 1 through 10 in the column designated as handicap strokes.

Both stroke play and match play may involve the incorporation of handicaps. In stroke play a player's handicap is subtracted from the total gross score and this results in the net score. In match play a stroke is subtracted from the gross score on each hole on which a player gets strokes to arrive at the net score for those holes.

If you become a member of a women's or men's group at a public or private course, an individual or a committee will figure your handicap, usually working through a computer service. When this is being done, it is important to post all of your scores along with the course ratings.

IMPORTANT RULES OF GOLF

The United States Golf Association and The Royal and Ancient Golf Club of St. Andrews, Scotland, approve "The Rules of Golf" which govern play. A small, inexpensive book called *The Rules of Golf* can be purchased from the shops at most public and private golf courses.* There is a new edition each year.

All players should have rule books to study and carry with them in their golf bags for reference when necessary. The following information on rules will give you a start toward learning about the many situations which call for decisions. This section will not contain all of the rules or substitute for your studying the official rules and conduct of experienced golfers.

The Rules of Golf may also be obtained from The Golf House, Far Hills, NJ 07931. A simplified presentation of the rules is found in *Easy Way to Learn Golf Rules*, National Golf Foundation, 200 Castlewood Street, North Palm Beach, FL 33408.

1. Playing the Ball As It Lies In the very early days, golf had only one rule. The player was not allowed to touch the ball except with a club from the time it was teed off until after it was holed out. This is still true with some exceptions:

a. Your ball may be marked and lifted when on the putting green for the purpose of cleaning it or if it interferes with the line of another player's putt.

b. A ball which has been damaged may be replaced.

c. A ball may be dropped into a new spot if it lands in "ground under repair," temporary or "casual water," or an animal hole. It may also be moved and dropped if it is within two club lengths of an immovable obstruction, such as a building, a stationary bench, a water fountain, etc., if they interfere with your swing (see no. 2).

d. There are other situations in which the ball cannot be played as it lies unless a penalty is taken. These will be described in subsequent sections.

e. Some local rules allow "winter rules" or "preferred lies" by which the ball may be moved to a better lie, usually within six inches. These rules are sometimes in effect because of difficult conditions on a course which may have been caused by heavy rains, spring thaws, etc. These rules are not part of "The Official Rules of Golf."

2. Dropping the Ball The correct way to drop a ball when it is allowed is to stand facing the hole and drop the ball over your shoulder so that it comes to rest within two club lengths of the spot where it is to land and no nearer the hole. If the ball rolls nearer to the hole because of a slope, you are allowed to place it. Also, if the ball must be moved for a legitimate reason on the putting green, it is placed rather than dropped.

3. Playing the Course As It Is You may not stamp down or rearrange the ground under or near your ball or move anything that is growing, such as a tree branch. You must play the course as it is, with some exceptions:

a. On the teeing area you may smooth out irregularities.

b. You may move loose impediments, which include natural objects such as leaves, small rocks, twigs, etc., from all places except from sand bunkers and water hazards.

c. Any place on the course you may move an obstruction which is interpreted to be an artificial object such as a rake, a bottle, a can, etc.

4. Teeing Off

a. On the first tee the player who hits first or has the honor is determined by lot. On subsequent holes the player with the lowest score has the honor. After teeing off the player farthest from the hole hits first.

b. You may tee off anywhere between the tee markers up to a depth of two club lengths behind them.

5. Playing on the Putting Green

a. If your ball hits the flagstick when putted, the penalty is two strokes in stroke play and loss of hole in match play.

b. You may not touch the putting line except to repair ball marks and move loose impediments.

c. In stroke play if your ball which is played from the green hits a fellow competitor's ball also on the green it is a two-stroke penalty and the displaced ball is changed to its original spot. In match play there is no penalty and your opponent may either play the ball from its new position or replace it.

d. If your ball lands on the incorrect green you may drop it off the green within two club lengths, and no nearer the hole. No penalty.

6. Ball in a Hazard

a. A hazard is a bunker (sometimes referred to as a sand trap) or a water hazard such as a lake, a brook, or a ditch and their banks.

b. If you attempt to hit your ball out of a hazard, you may not ground your club. You may not touch the ground, sand, or water with the club until the forward swing is made.

c. If your ball goes into a water hazard and you cannot play it out, you may: (1) drop a ball any distance behind the hazard in line with the hole and the point it entered the hazard or (2) you may hit a ball again from the original place. In both situations the penalty is one stroke.

d. If your ball enters a lateral water hazard (one which runs parallel to the line of play) you may drop a ball on either side of the hazard, within two club lengths, and opposite the point at which the ball entered the hazard, not nearer the hole. The penalty is one stroke.

7. Ball Out of Bounds

a. A ball is considered out of bounds when all of the ball is in an area usually marked by out-of-bounds stakes or a fence. In this situation you either drop a ball from the place where you hit the ball that went out of bounds or, if it was your first shot, hit another ball from the tee. The penalty is one stroke and loss of distance. (If your tee shot goes out of bounds, you are hitting "3" from the tee, so you add a penalty stroke and lose the original distance from the tee.)

b. If you are not sure whether your ball is out of bounds, it is well to hit a provisional ball. If it is out of bounds, you continue play with the provisional ball. If not, you continue with your original ball.

8. Lost Ball Follow the same procedure and apply the same penalty as for out of bounds if you cannot find your ball. You are allowed up to five minutes to look for your ball. Penalty for a lost ball is one stroke and loss of distance.

9. Unplayable Lie If your ball lands in a place in which you feel you cannot hit it, you may call it an unplayable lie (except in a water hazard). You are the only one who can judge your ball unplayable. If you do so, you have the following options:

a. You may take the original shot again.
b. You may drop the ball within two club lengths, but not nearer the hole.
c. You may drop the ball anywhere behind the original lie which keeps it between you and the hole.

The penalty in all cases is one stroke and also loss of distance on the first option.

There are many other situations in golf for which rules exist. The general penalty for not complying with a rule is loss of hole in match play and two strokes in stroke play. There are many differences in penalties, however, so as you become more serious about the game it is important that you check the official rule book. Knowing and applying the rules will help you avoid embarrassing situations, will promote good golf habits, and will often save strokes.

PLAYING A TYPICAL GOLF HOLE

In order to apply some of the knowledge in this chapter to the playing of a typical hole, you may find the following hypothetical situation helpful; refer to Figure 5.2 as you read. (Note: In order to explain some of the penalty situations, the golfers experienced more trouble than might usually be the case.)

1. *Jack* scored lower on the previous hole and will have the honor at the tee. Since the men's teeing area is farther back on this hole, he would tee off first for safety reasons even though he did not have the honor. Jack tees up his ball between the markers and drives it out of bounds on the right. He can definitely see that it went out of bounds and deep into the woods. He must then hit another ball. Since he is penalized stroke and distance for hitting out of bounds, he is now hitting "3" from the tee. This shot lands in the middle of the fairway about 210 yards out.

2. *Mary* moves forward to the women's teeing area, takes out her driver, and tees the ball up between the markers. The distance of the hole from the women's tee is 383 yards. She drives her ball about 175 yards down the left side of the fairway.

3. Since *Mary* is still away, or further from the hole than Jack, she walks to her ball and hits again. This time she uses a #3 wood. She mis-hits the shot, and her ball dribbles into the lake.

4. *Jack* decides not to delay play by trying to find his first ball, since it went deep into a heavily wooded area. He uses his #3 wood and hits a shot which lands to the left of the green and in the sand bunker. He is now lying "4."

5. *Mary* finds her ball in the lake and retrieves it. She finds a level spot behind the lake, faces the hole, and drops her ball over her shoulder. She must count a stroke for hitting her ball into the lake, so she is now lying "3." She takes out her #9 and hits an approach shot to the putting green.

6. *Jack* finds his ball in the bunker and takes out his #9 iron, since he does not have a wedge in his set. He sets up to his shot and is careful not to ground the club. He hits a good explosion shot which lands fairly close to the flagstick. He smooths out the sand trap with the rake when he finishes his shot and replaces the rake in the trap.

7. *Mary* is farthest from the flagstick, so she will putt first. *Jack* is in her line and marks his ball. *Mary* can see the hole clearly, so *Jack* removes the flagstick and carefully lays it on the green. *Mary* makes a good putt,

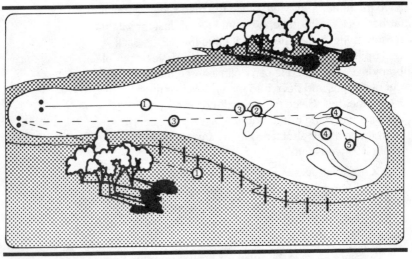

Figure 5.2 *A par-4, 410-yard hold (Jack—broken line; Mary—solid line).*

and her ball finishes 6 inches from the hole. To speed up play, she putts out rather than marking her ball. She finishes the hole with a double bogey 6.

8. *Jack* lines up his putt while *Mary* quietly watches. He sinks his putt and also finishes with a double bogey 6. He then replaces the flagstick.

9. *Jack* and *Mary* pick up their clubs, which they had placed off the green on the side closest to the next teeing area, and quickly walk toward the next tee. They will record their scores there as they wait for the group ahead of them to be well out of range.

6

MENTAL ASPECTS OF GOLF

Throughout golf literature the importance of the mental aspects of golf have been stressed along with repeated practice of the mechanical skills. In fact, writers and players have said that from 60 to 90 percent of the game is mental. Obviously, the possession of fundamental skills cannot be minimized, especially for the beginning golfer. If your grip is incorrect and your swing pattern has serious errors, you will not have good results no matter how positive and productive your thoughts and attitudes might be. However, once you begin to improve and become somewhat consistent with the fundamentals, it is the mental aspects of your play which will make the big difference in how much you achieve and how much you enjoy the game. Although there are no magical answers to the mental side of golf, the ideas which follow should be of help as you practice and play the game.

DEVELOP POSITIVE ATTITUDES

Positive attitudes can help you at any stage of learning because they block out the negative thoughts and direct your thinking and attention to potentially good shots and good rounds. It is impossible to replay bad shots; those shots are gone forever, so you might as well plan for the next shot and try to think positively about how it will turn out. If you think your ball is going to land in the water, it probably will, for often a shot ends up the way you're thinking. It is easy to become discouraged about this elusive game, but discouragement does not help unless it somehow motivates you to practice and correct some of your mechanical and mental faults. Because golf is a relatively slow game there is plenty of time between shots to either forget the bad ones or remember the good ones. Try to make walking down the fairway to your ball a pleasant experience, one that will help you get ready for your next shot.

If you're an inexperienced golfer or a high handicapper, you're going to have a number of bad shots and bad scores. If you're trying your best at the moment, that's all you can do. Built into the whole concept of a positive attitude are attributes such as patience, persistence, calmness, and confidence. Of course, confidence without a certain amount of proficiency is very difficult to maintain, but practice and experience will help you gain the confidence which assists you in developing positive attitudes. Do anything that helps you approach the game positively—talk to yourself, talk to your ball, enjoy the scenery—but keep your thinking in a positive vein. Whether you have a bad round or a good one, there will be another day and another chance to try again.

ACCEPT YOUR OWN ABILITY

One of the difficult things to do in any sport is to be

honest with yourself and to accept your own ability. Setting a level of aspiration is tricky because it should be high enough to make you work but not so high that you become too frustrated and want to quit. Being realistic and making the best of what you have is important in golf. Because you play every shot yourself you must accept the responsibility for the result. It's tempting to blame the course or the behavior of others in your group, but ultimately you're the one who made the shot.

During practice is the time to try different kinds of shots, but on the course it's usually more successful to try shots within your range of ability. If you have never hit the ball 160 yards in practice with your #3 wood, the chance of your doing it on a course with an intervening water hazard is very remote. Some days your swing will be different from what it is in practice and you'll have to go with what you have. You may have to select a club or two higher to accomplish the result you wish. It is frequently stated by golf professionals that under-clubbing is one of the most common errors that golfers make. Try not to worry about what the other player can do with a particular club. Select the club you need on the basis of your own ability. Be aware of how far you generally hit the ball with each club and make your selection on the course accordingly. If you're the type of player who does not hit a very long ball with your woods, then compensate by working diligently on your short game and become as accurate with your irons and your putter as you can. Be aware of your own ability and accept it for what it is, and you and those you play with will have a much more pleasant and satisfying time on the golf course.

CONTROL YOUR EMOTIONS

Because golf is such an unpredictable game in which things can go well one moment and poorly the next, it is often a severe test of emotional control. However, if you keep the game in perspective and try to remember that any emotion you display on the course should be a mature and controlled response and should fit the situation, the golf round will usually turn out better. There are many more important things in life than a dubbed shot or a missed putt.

Many professional players have set an example for the ordinary golfer by displaying the value of an even temperament. A number of our fine players consciously try to maintain some kind of a balance between the emotions they show for good and bad shots. Anger over one bad shot can frequently result in two or three or a number of poor shots in addition to creating an unpleasant playing atmosphere for others in the group. Getting so angry that you throw a club can be dangerous, embarrassing, and destructive to your game. Your playing companions will quickly forget and excuse your high score, but they will not so readily forget inappropriate behavior.

Another emotion which sometimes takes hold of golfers is the fear of doing poorly—of hitting the ball into the sand or the ravine, of hitting the ball out of bounds. This type of fear is not unusual, especially for the less experienced and less skillful golfer. Some solutions for dealing with this kind of fear are to take more club than you normally do and to try to slow down your swing, since fear often causes you to hurry. Usually the best solution is to practice the kinds of shots you're afraid of so that you will be a little better prepared and more confident the next time you face those situations.

Above all, humility and a sense of humor will make a better situation out of a poor one on the golf course. As has been said many times, golf is a great promoter of humility and sometimes the only way out is to grin and bear what's happening. Some days you seem to be able to sink those putts so easily and other days even the short ones don't go into the cup. Maintaining a sense of humor doesn't mean that you make light of everything that goes wrong, but it will help you not to take yourself and the game too seriously.

CONCENTRATE

All golfers who expect to accomplish some degree of proficiency must cultivate the mental skill of concentration, or of close mental application to the task they are attempting. Actually, the periods of concentration come in relatively short spurts in golf and are less tiring than in some sports. On the other hand, because there are large spaces of time between shots the mind also has a greater chance to wander than in many sports. If you're thinking about what you did on the last hole or what you have to do at work as you're approaching your shot, the result may not turn out very well. Good general advice is to play one shot at a time and block out all distractions which might inhibit that shot. Along with concentrating on each shot, you should play your own game and not let the play of others distract or bother you. If you play the golf course and not the other player, you are more likely to maintain better concentration. There are some people, however, who are motivated to concentrate better if they are competing against the score of another player. You should be aware of the kind of player you are and direct your thoughts accordingly.

One important guideline as you play a round of golf is to concentrate on the target you're hitting toward rather than on the detailed mechanics of your swing. Cluttering your mind with all kinds of do's and don'ts about your swing as you are set up for your shot or as you swing at the ball can do more to inhibit your swing than to aid it. The time to analyze your swing and work on details is on the practice tee, not on the course. If you think about your swing at all as you are about to hit the ball, the advice most teachers give is to think large key thoughts about your total swing. Ernest Jones, one of our great teachers in golf, expresses his main concept in the title he gave his third book, *Swing the Clubhead*. All of these ideas are clues which may or may not help you find your own best way to concentrate. There are no absolutes that work for everyone, and as you play and experiment you will find what works best for you and your game.

VISUALIZE YOUR SHOTS

A mental preparation which has been used extensively in golf is visualization of a shot before it is hit. Seeing a mental moving picture of the shot almost as though the individual were watching television has been practiced in different ways by many of our great golfers, including Ben Hogan, Sam Snead, and Arnold Palmer. In *Golf My Way*, Jack Nicklaus describes the visual process he goes through before he selects a club and steps up to his ball. First he sees where he wants the ball to finish. Then he visualizes the trajectory of the shot and how it lands, and finally he sees the kind of swing he will make to achieve the mental picture of the shot. This process has been very beneficial in producing successful results for him most of the time.

One of the major ideas behind the visualization process is to help the player gain confidence in what he is about to attempt. This technique can be tried on the practice tee as well as on the course so that the players can gain skill in the imaginative process. Obviously, you must be somewhat realistic about your own ability in the kind of shot you visualize. The mental picture need not be a spectacular shot if your capabilities cannot produce this, but at least it can be a picture of a positive and trouble-free shot.

Some teachers and golfers have suggested that there is value in visualizing and practicing good shots in your mind when you're not on the course. This approach is referred to as mental practice. As reported in research literature dealing with the learning of motor skills, mental practice has produced some positive learning results, especially when combined with actual practice. Also related to the visualization process is the ability to watch good golfers on television or in person and to attempt to retain these positive swing images in your mind for later use. How you use the various aspects of the visualization process and how valuable they will be for you can only be determined as you practice and try them.

SOME FINAL THOUGHTS

The ideas presented in this chapter may help you in channeling your mental energy to your best advantage. If you lack experience, you can often help the mental part of your game by not trying too hard and by approaching the shot and the game a little more casually. Even after you become more experienced and consistent you may find times when you are playing a great deal but you seem to be stale and in a slump. At this point some time off and an entire change of pace may improve your mental outlook and your game.

7

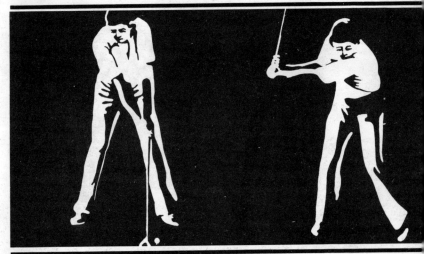

CORRECTING COMMON ERRORS

The most common errors in the game have not
changed over the years. Topping, scuffing, slicing,
hooking, and shanking have persisted in providing
the greatest amount of trouble for the average player.
Fortunately, few players experience all of these at the
same time, but chances are good that you will
experience most of them at some time.

Many players choose to accept these problems as
part of the game and seem to be content to live with
them. Others would sincerely like to be rid of them, but
simply don't know how to go about it. By understanding
the cause of these errant shots and the mechanical

adjustments needed for their correction, you should be able to analyze your own swing and make the necessary adjustments to rapidly improve your game.

Basic to the correction of all swing errors is a fundamentally sound swing pattern that is consistent. In other words, until your body is "programmed" to consistently execute the elements of the swing in the proper sequence and with correct timing, the result will be a variety of mis-hit shots like those described in this chapter.

TOPPING

A topped shot occurs when the clubhead makes contact with only the top half of the ball. This can be done in two different ways: (1) bringing the clubhead straight down into the ball or (2) catching the top half of the ball as the clubhead is on its way up in the start of the follow-through.

The following swing errors all contribute to the problem of topping. Some of these may be obvious to you, but often a player won't be able to recognize his/her swing errors without the help of an observer.

Ball Too Far Forward or Back at Address

Playing the ball too far forward can result in contacting it on the upswing and playing it too far back to chopping down on top of it.
CORRECTION: Position the ball where the clubhead will make contact just before it starts moving upward.

Tension

When the muscles are tense and the club is gripped too tightly, it often results in a shortened swing radius and jerky movement through the ball.
CORRECTION: Take a relaxed grip at position of address, keep swing smooth and under control.

Faulty Weight Distribution

It is likely that the clubhead will contact the top half of the ball on the way up if more weight is on the right foot at impact than there was at the position of address. On the other hand, if the weight is kept on the left foot throughout the swing or too much weight is thrown to the left side, the body will be too far forward when the ball is contacted, causing the clubhead to hit down into the ball.
CORRECTION: Be sure a smooth weight transfer (not too excessive) takes place from the right foot to the left before striking the ball.

Swaying to the Right or Left

The head and upper body should not move laterally in either direction during the swing. This action will bring the same results as a faulty weight transfer.

CORRECTION: Maintain a steady head position throughout the swing.

Raising Up

The head and shoulders should not be allowed to raise up before the ball is contacted. This error is brought about in three ways: (1) raising from the trunk, (2) stiffening the right leg at the top of the backswing, and (3) straightening the left knee prior to impact. All of these can cause the clubhead to be too high at impact.

CORRECTION: Be sure the head and shoulders remain level and keep both knees slightly flexed throughout the swing.

Bending Left Elbow

Bending the left elbow on the backswing and trying to return it to the straight position at impact leads to topping because the ball is often contacted before the elbow has completely straightened.

CORRECTION: Maintain a firm left arm throughout the swing.

SCUFFING

Scuffing, or hitting "fat," is simply hitting the ground with your club before contacting the ball. This will not only cause a lack of distance, but will also destroy the backspin action desired on your approach shots.

Scuffing generally occurs when the hands deliver the clubhead before the legs and hips have made their move in the downswing. Several factors contribute to this problem.

Reverse Weight Transfer

When the left knee is allowed to bend too much on the backswing, it puts the weight on the left foot and encourages a reverse weight transfer on the downswing. That is, the weight transfers from the left foot to the right, which is the reverse of what is desired. With the weight in this position it will be extremely difficult to keep the clubhead from making contact with the ground behind the intended spot.

CORRECTION: Make sure your left knee moves toward the right and only slightly down in the backswing (see Chapter 2). Initiate the downswing with the legs and hips, and transfer the weight from right to left foot before contacting the ball.

Collapsing Right Side

Even with a correct weight transfer, "fat" shots will result when the right side bends too severely on the downswing, allowing the right shoulder to drop lower than at address.

CORRECTION: Maintain head and shoulders at the same level throughout the swing.

Swinging from the Top

Of the various causes of scuffing, swinging from the top ranks highest on the list. It occurs when the right hand takes over at the top of the backswing and literally pushes the clubhead down into the ground. There are four basic causes that prompt this action: (1) only a partial shoulder turn in the backswing, (2) having the weight on the left foot at the top of the backswing, (3) swinging too fast, and (4) trying to "kill" the ball.

CORRECTION: Be sure to make a full shoulder turn and have the weight on the right instep at the top of the backswing. Slow down the backswing and let the left arm pull the club through. Don't overswing!

SLICING

Few will disagree that more players are plagued with the slice than any other error in the game. This shot either starts out on line and breaks sharply to the right, or it starts out left and curves back toward the center of the fairway. In either case, the direct cause is an open clubface at impact. In the first instance, the clubhead is moving down the target line at impact, which starts the ball out straight; but because the clubface is open,

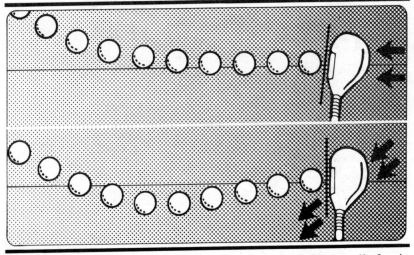

Figure 7.1 *Normal slice (above).*   Figure 7.2 *Pull slice (below).*

clockwise spin is imparted to the ball, causing it to make a sharp turn to the right (see Figure 7.1). In the latter case, the clubhead is moving from the outside across the target line, causing the ball to start out left of target. With the clubface being open to the flight path of the club (see Figure 7.2), the clockwise spin will again bring the ball back to the right.

Another type of shot which is somewhat related to the slice—because it ends up right of the target— is the "push" shot. It occurs when the clubhead is moving across the target line from the inside and the clubface is facing the same direction. Since it is not nearly as common or troublesome as the slice, all that will be said about it is to get the clubhead traveling down the target line sooner.

The following are the most common errors that produce a slice, with some suggested corrections.

Faulty Grip

Slicing action is encouraged when the hands are placed too far to the left on the club. Having the hands in this position will almost always cause the clubface to open too much during the backswing and to remain open at impact. Also, gripping the club too tightly with the right hand or "grabbing" during the downswing will prevent the clubface from squaring to the target.

CORRECTION: Move the hands to the right so that the V's formed by the thumbs and forefingers point at the right shoulder. Maintain light grip pressure with the right hand throughout the swing.

Improper Alignment

A common alignment error is to address the ball with the shoulders lined up left of the target line. This alignment sets up the outside-in swing path, with the usual slice result.

CORRECTION: Set up at address with the feet, knees, hips, and shoulders parallel to the target line. If the outside-in swing persists, close your stance some by dropping the right foot back from the target line.

Ball Placement

Placing the ball right of the center of your stance often results in contacting the ball before the clubhead has had a chance to square to the target. This action will produce the shot shown in Figure 7.1. If the ball is positioned too far forward, your club will already be starting back to the inside at impact which can result in either a slice or a pull-slice.

CORRECTION: The best ball position for most golfers is opposite the inner left heel. A small variation could work better for some, but it should be very slight.

Pulling Across the Body

Pulling across the body with the arms forces the clubface to "cut across" the ball and send the club left of the target too soon in the follow-through.

CORRECTION: Keep left arm moving down the target line at least a foot on the follow-through before allowing the club to start back to the left.

Incomplete Shoulder Turn

Another common cause of an outside-in swing path is related to a partial shoulder turn at the top of the backswing. This position makes it almost impossible for the club to start the downswing on an inside path which will result in the same slice pattern.

CORRECTION: Be conscious of making a full shoulder turn at the top of the backswing (see Chapter 2).

Forward Movement of Upper Body

If the head and shoulders are allowed to move forward before impact, the hands will always be late in squaring the clubface. The result can only be more sliced shots.

CORRECTION: Concentrate on keeping the head behind the ball until after impact.

HOOKING

The hook is not nearly as common as the slice, and it is generally much easier to correct. A hooked shot has just the opposite action from the slice. It can either start out straight toward the target and curve sharply left (see Figure 7.3), or start out left of the target and curve even farther left (see Figure 7.4).

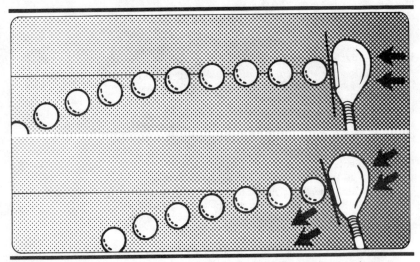

Figure 7.3 *Hook (above).*   **Figure 7.4** *Pull hook (below).*

The hooking action in Figure 7.3 is a result of the clubface being closed at impact even though the clubhead path is on the target line. The closed clubface imparts a counterclockwise spin on the ball, causing it to curve to the left.

The ball starts out left in Figure 7.4 because the clubhead path comes across the target line from the outside. With the clubface in a closed position, the resulting counterclockwise spin will cause the ball to curve even farther left.

The shot that goes straight left is called a "pull" shot.

The clubhead path is the same as with the pull hook (outside in), but the clubface at impact is facing in the direction the clubhead is moving rather than being closed. All that is needed to straighten this shot is to get the clubhead moving down the target line.

The following are the most common errors related to hooking with suggested corrections.

Faulty Grip

The natural position of the hands at impact is for the back of the left hand and the palm of the right to be facing the target. Thus when the club is held with the hands too far to the right on the club at address, the clubface will usually arrive at impact with a closed face, causing a hook.

CORRECTION: Move hands to the left so that the V's formed by the

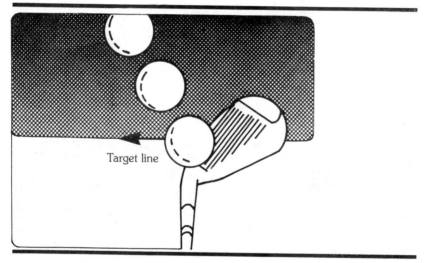

Target line

Figure 7.5   Shank

forefinger and thumbs point to the right eye (see Chapter 2). This should offset the tendency to turn the clubface to the left too soon.

Incorrect Alignment

Many golfers address the ball with a closed stance which aligns the body to the right of the target. This alignment forces the clubhead path to come from inside the target line, and if the hands are in the correct position at impact (square to the target) the clubface will be closed, resulting in a hook.

CORRECTION: Square up your stance so that the shoulders point left of the target but are parallel to the target line (see Chapter 2).

Ball Positioned Too Far Back or Forward

When the ball is positioned too far back in the stance, the clubface will contact the ball from the inside before it has started down the target line. If the clubface is square to the target line at this early impact, a hooking action will result.

When the ball is too far forward, it may be contacted after the clubhead has left the target line and started back to the left. The result will be either a pull or a hook, depending on whether the clubface is square to the clubhead path or closed to it.

Right-Hand Domination

A dominant right hand can cause a hook as well as other errors previously discussed. When the right hand takes over the downswing, the clubhead will usually be thrown outside the target line, producing an outside-in swing. The overactive right hand often causes the wrists to "roll" as well, and when this happens a pulled hook is almost a certainty.

CORRECTION: Let the left arm and side dominate the downswing and maintain only light grip pressure with the right hand. Keep a firm left wrist at impact. Don't overswing!

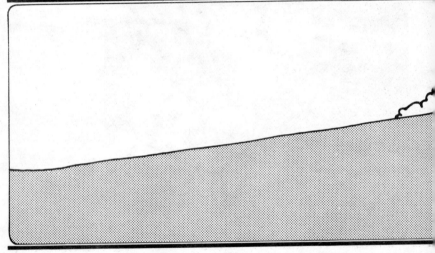

SHANKING

Shanking is probably the most devasting of all the problem shots in golf. It can happen to players at all levels, but is much more common with the beginner. When a ball is shanked it flies to the right, almost at right angles to the target. It occurs when the path of the club on the downswing puts the clubhead entirely outside the ball at impact, causing the ball to be contacted on the hosel (see Figure 7.5).

The swing errors that identify with shanking, along with suggested corrections, are as follows:

Faulty Backswing

A poorly executed backswing is a major cause of throwing or shoving the clubhead out beyond the ball. Taking the club back too far to the inside or outside of the target line, grabbing with the right hand, restricting the shoulder turn, overswinging, and swinging too fast will all contribute to a shank.

CORRECTION: Grip the club with light pressure throughout the swing and avoid "grabbing" with the right hand on the way back. The first foot or so of the takeaway should be straight back on the target line. Make a slow, smooth backswing with a full shoulder turn at the top (see Chapter 2). Let the left arm lead the downswing, and don't overswing!

Falling Forward on the Toes

Many times the execution of the swing itself is reasonably sound, but the player's body is allowed to fall forward slightly, putting the clubhead outside the ball at impact. In any event, it's almost a certainty that when the ball is shanked, the weight will be too far forward on the toes.

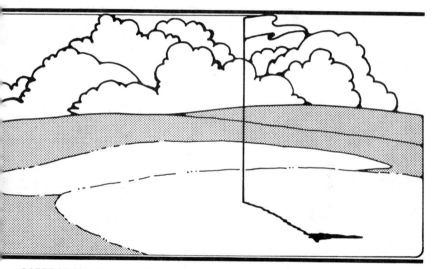

CORRECTION: Set up at address with the weight more on the balls of the feet rather than toward the heels. During the downswing make a very slight weight shift back toward the heels. This will offset the somewhat natural tendency to fall forward.

8

PRACTICE, PLAYING, AND CONDITIONING IDEAS

Purposeful practice and playing are important if you expect to improve. Too often the beginning golfer goes to a driving range or a practice field and hits balls one right after the other. Rapidly hitting a large number of balls will not automatically increase your proficiency. A more useful practice would be to approximate as closely as possible the different kinds of shots you would generally experience on the golf course. Also, practicing is sometimes confused with warming up for a playing round. According to many golf professionals, the best time to practice is *after* you have played. In whatever way you are best able to fit practicing and playing into your own time schedule, the following ideas should help you plan and be more thoughtful about your practice and playing sessions.

PRACTICE HINTS AND IDEAS

• Practice all phases of your game, not just your strengths. Review fundamentals.

• On a practice area or a driving range, start your practice with the short irons and gradually move up to the driver. Work on every club in your bag or on every club you have had some experience with in your lessons.

• Be sure you have a goal in mind. Aim for a target and then strive for consistency. Many driving ranges have markers you can hit toward, or you can use a ball, a bare spot in the grass, or some identifiable area; on a field you can use old towels as targets (they can be anchored with golf tees if it's windy). If you are on a field rather than a driving range, simply move back as you progress to the longer clubs and leave the target where it is.

• Carefully observe how far you usually hit each club. Use yardage markers at a driving range or either measure or pace off distances on a field.

• Save enough time to work on the parts of your game which give you the most trouble.

• Watch the flight of the balls you hit. Then try to determine what kind of changes you must make to achieve your purpose.

• Become familiar with wind and its effect on the flight of the ball. Practice hitting balls from different directions if there is wind.

• Take time between your shots. Plan and visualize each shot.

• Practice from grass, if available. Hit balls from good lies and poor lies so that you will experience situations you will find on a course. If you have trouble with fairway lies, use a tee until you gain confidence or correct your swing errors.

- Practice swinging some without a ball, particularly if you need to develop more freedom in swinging through the ball. Take some practice swings after a poor shot.

- Practice from bunkers (sand traps) and grass which approximates the rough on a golf course, if available. Trouble shots are especially difficult in actual play if you don't have a chance to practice them.

- After you have hit with each club, try practicing as though you were playing on a course. Use a scorecard and actually play different-length holes from the practice tee.

- Spend enough time on putting. Start with short putts which you can see and hear drop into the cup. Move to longer putts, always trying to get the ball into the hole in two putts. Try uphill, downhill, and sidehill putts to become acquainted with all different types of contours.

- Practice alone when possible, but if you are with others try to minimize conversation and maximize concentration.

- Frequent short practice sessions are usually better than a fewer number of long ones. As you become more experienced, practice sessions can be lengthened. Try to persist to the extent that you increase your mental and playing endurance.

- If you wish to become a good golfer, find time to practice and develop a balanced schedule between practice and actual play.

- Try not to be disappointed if the practice does not immediately improve your golf on the course. The two situations are different, and sometimes you may have a particularly bad round after practicing something new. Old habits are difficult to break.

- Apply the performance and mental concepts you have studied to your practice sessions and you should gradually make progress. Remember—it takes time to develop a good golf swing.

PLAYING HINTS AND STRATEGY

- Slow down your pace before you go out for an actual round of golf. Arrive early for your tee-off time. Avoid all possibilities of approaching your round in a hurried state, if you can.

- Warm up by hitting a small number of balls. The purpose of the warm-up is to loosen up, build confidence, and become more acquainted with the terrain and the putting green. Be sure to include chipping and putting.

- If you are a beginner, try to play with someone who is experienced on a course, especially the first two or three times. This person will be able to help you with the application of etiquette and rules. If your play becomes slow, however, do not apply all the rules. Improve your lie if necessary, but work toward playing the ball as it lies.

- If you are inexperienced, start course play on a par-3 course or play less than eighteen holes. Gradually work toward more holes and more difficult courses.

- Avoid taking or giving a lesson on the course unless your round is specifically for that purpose. Most professional teachers will give playing lessons when their schedule and course play allows for the time.

- Try to swing at the ball as you do in practice. Stay with basic fundamentals. As stressed earlier in the chapter on mental aspects, concentrate on why and where you are hitting rather than on the details of your swing.

- Your primary concerns should be to keep the ball in play and to avoid trouble areas on the course. "Play safe" and allow for some range of error in your shots.

- Pick up a scorecard early if you are playing a new course. Learn as much as you can from it before you go out on the course. Check the local rules on the card, which will apply only to that course.

- In deciding what club to use for a particular shot, consider (1) distance, (2) the lie of your ball, (3) course conditions, (4) weather conditions, and (5) the topography of the course.

- Watch how the course and weather conditions affect other players' shots. In an official tournament or match you may not ask advice of an opponent, but you can intelligently observe what is happening to their shots. Watch a putt that is similar to the one you will be hitting. Watch how wind affects someone else's ball. Watch how the terrain affects the roll of the ball.

- Inquire whether there are specific trees, bushes, or lines on cart paths which indicate specific distances to the green from certain areas. Many courses have a specific kind of bush or tree which indicates when you are 150 yards away from the center of the green. Also, many courses have yardage-guide cards in addition to the score card, which show landmarks on the course and their distances from the green.

- Even though you become intelligent about yardage markings on a course you will find that judging distance is a matter of experience. Small depressions and valleys on the course can make a hole appear shorter than it is.

- If you know approximately what distance you usually hit with a particular club, this knowledge will help you plan your shots.

- Some holes "dogleg"—bend to the left or to the right. In general, if a hole bends to the left, you should aim for the right side of the fairway and vice versa. In this way you give yourself a better chance for a clear shot to the green.

- Often the placement of your shot is more important than distance. For example, if there is a hazard between you and the green and two of your normal shots would put you into it, take less club on your first two shots so that you land behind the hazard on your second shot.

- Once you have played a course try to recall as much about it as you can when you play it again. The more experienced you become the more you will remember.

- As you become more experienced, keep a record of various aspects of your game, such as number of putts, number of greens hit in regulation or one or two over regulation—whatever your goal might be. (Since par allows for two putts, regulation on a par 3 is one stroke; on par 4, two strokes; and on par 5, three strokes.) Also, keep track of how many shots were wasted because of penalty shots and mental errors.

- Evaluate your round when you finish. Identify where you had most of your difficulties so that you can intelligently plan your next practice session. If possible, practice some immediately after you finish a round. Remember—that round is over. Learn what you can from it and get ready for the next one.

CONDITIONING IDEAS AND SUGGESTIONS

The physical requirements related to golf are often deceiving to the beginner. It's true that playing a round of golf doesn't place the physical demands on its players that more vigorous activities do. However, it's quite common to see players start out well on the front nine and completely fall apart on the back side due to fatigue. A level of endurance that will allow you to walk the course without tiring will make the game more enjoyable and result in lower scores as well.

Along with endurance, some players could benefit greatly from added strength and/or flexibility. If the body is not flexible enough to make a full shoulder turn and proper hip rotation, the clubhead speed will be retarded resulting in loss of distance. Also, many players (particularly among women) simply lack the strength in the legs and upper body to attain distance on their shots. It should be emphasized, however, that developing a fundamentally sound swing will be far more beneficial in achieving greater distance than will working for additional strength.

The following exercises are recommended to those who feel a need to become better conditioned in any or all three of these areas.

Endurance

Your choice of the activities suggested below should be participated in on a daily basis.

- Walking briskly, especially over hilly terrain.
- Jogging at a moderate pace.

- Bicycling (if using a 10-speed, set gears where peddling at a fast pace will be required).
- Swimming.
- Step-up exercise. Use a stool or bench approximately 18″ high. Step up and down with both feet some 30 times per minute. Start out conservatively and increase the time as your endurance increases.

Flexibility

These exercises should be done by moving smoothly to the point of stress (avoid bouncing) and holding for eight seconds. Relax and repeat as often as your condition will allow. Benefits are in direct

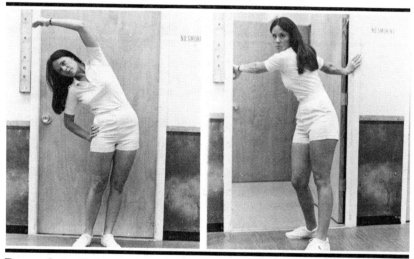

Figure 8.1 *Sides*   **Figure 8.2** *Shoulders and sides*

proportion to the frequency of performance.

Sides. Stand with your legs shoulder-width apart. Bend to one side, reaching overhead with opposite arm. Hold and return to upright position, then repeat on other side. (Figure 8.1.)

Shoulders and Sides. Stand facing a doorway as far away as your arm reach will allow. With your arms fully extended, grasp the doorjamb with both hands and make a quarter turn to the left with your feet. Keep your head turned to the left and rotate your left shoulder up under your chin. Pull with your left

Figure 8.3 *Lower back*

arm and push with your right and hold. Reverse the direction to the right and repeat. (Figure 8.2.)

Lower Back. While lying on your back with your arms extended out at shoulder level, bring your right leg up and over to touch your left hand. Hold while keeping as much of your back on the floor as possible. Return to the starting position and repeat on other side. (Figure 8.3.)

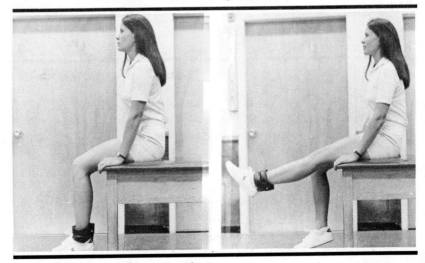

Figure 8.4 *Lower leg extensions*

Strength

Ideally, these exercises should be done in two to three sets of eight to twelve repetitions three times a week. The amount of weight used should be adjusted so that maximum effort is required with each set. *Caution: Weight exercises should be supervised to avoid misuse of weights and injury.*

Lower Leg Extensions. If a leg machine is not available, sit at the end of a table, bench, or tall chair. Strap a small weight to your foot and raise your leg so that it is completely extended in front of you. Exercise only one leg at a time to prevent the stronger leg from dominating. (Figure 8.4.)

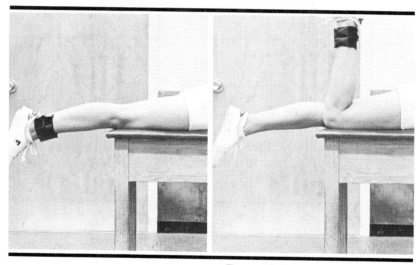

Figure 8.5 *Lower leg flexions*

Lower Leg Flexions. With a weight strapped to your foot (approximately one-third of that used in leg extensions), lie face down on a table or floor. From a straight-leg position, bend your leg one half to two-thirds of the way to your buttocks and return. (Figure 8.5.)

Arm Extensions. Lie face down on a bench with your arms extended at shoulder level. Using very light dumbbell weights, raise your arms 12″ to 18″ and return to the starting position. Don't bend your elbows, and be careful not to arch your back. (Figure 8.6.)

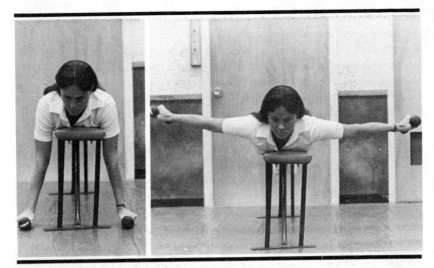

Figure 8.6 *Arm extensions*

Upright Rowing. Using light barbell weights to begin with, grasp bar near the center with your hands approximately 6″ apart. Standing up straight with the bar balanced, lift the barbell along the front of your body to a point beneath your chin and return to starting position. Keep your elbows high. (Figure 8.7.)

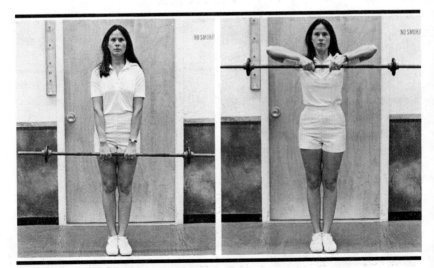

Figure 8.7 *Upright rowing*

Figure 8.8 *Pull-ups*

Pull-ups. Using a bar secured at reach height, grasp the
bar in overhand position and pull your body up to
where your chin touches the bar. Return to starting
position, and repeat as many times as you can.
(Figure 8.8.)

Golf Swing with Pulley. If pulley weights are
accessible, they can provide an excellent exercise

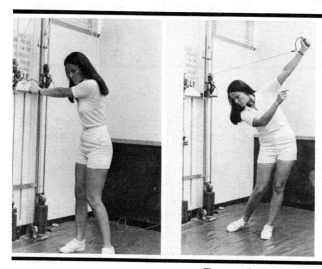

Figure 8.9 *Golf swing with pulley*

which approximates the golf swing. Stand with your "back" shoulder nearest the pulley and assume the position you would normally have at the top of your backswing. Grasp the pulley with your left hand and pull it through the full range of the downswing and follow-through. Use your legs and hips as though you were actually swinging at a ball. Again, the amount of weight should be adjusted with each set so that eight to twelve repetitions will require maximum effort. Alternate sets, using your left and right hands separately, and then both hands together. (Figure 8.9.)

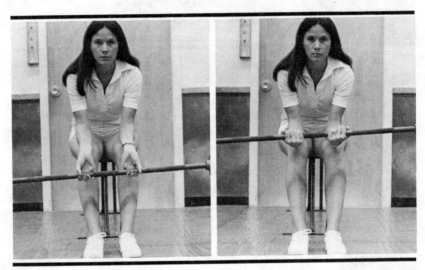

Figure 8.10   *Forearm curl*

Forearm Curl. While seated on a bench or chair, grasp the barbell (no attached weights are needed) at shoulder width while supporting your forearms on your thighs. Extend your fingers, allowing the bar to roll downward, and bring the bar back by flexing your fingers. (Figure 8.10.)

9

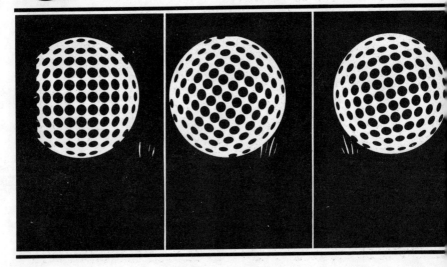

TERMINOLOGY OF GOLF

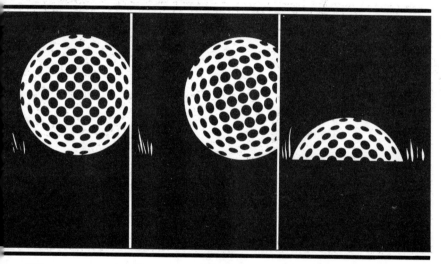

 s in other chapters of this book, terms designating right and left apply to right-handed golfers.

Ace

A slang expression for a hole-in-one.

Address

The player's position before the swing is taken.

Advice

Suggestions which could influence a player selecting a club, in swinging at the ball, or in making decisions about playing strategy.

Approach

A shot to the putting green, not made from the teeing ground.

Apron

The area just adjacent to the putting green. It is cut shorter than the fairway grass but not as short as the putting-green grass.

Away

The ball which is farthest from the flagstick and next to be played.

Back Door

A description for a putt which rolls around the cup and falls in from the rear.

Back Nine

The second nine holes of an eighteen-hole golf course.

Backspin

A reverse spin imparted to the ball which causes it to stop quickly upon landing.

Banana Ball

A slang term for a shot which curves wildly from left to right.

Barranca

A Spanish term for a deep ravine.

Best Ball

A match in which one golfer plays against the better ball of two players or the best ball of three players.

Birdie

A score of one stroke under par for a hole.

Bite

The backspin on the ball which causes it to stop quickly or bounce and roll backward upon landing.

Blade

Description of a putter with a thin head.

Blind

Description of a hole when the putting green cannot be seen by a player making a normal approach shot.

Bogey

A score of one stroke over par on a hole.

Brassie

The #2 wood. Seldom included in a matched set of clubs today.

Break

The sideways curving or slant of the putting green.

Bunker

A hazard or a depressed area filled with sand. In common usage called a sand trap. Bunker is a Scottish word for a large bin.

Caddie

Someone who carries a player's clubs. A caddie may give advice to the player.

Casual Water

An accumulation of water which is temporary. Not considered a water hazard.

Chip Shot

A short, low approach shot to the putting green. Usually consists of minimum carry and maximum roll.

Closed Face

The clubface pointing to the left of the intended target. Sometimes incorrectly referred to as tilting the clubface forward.

Closed Stance

The left foot is closer to the intended line of flight than the right foot.

Clubface

The normal striking surface of the head of the club.

Course Rating

The difficulty rating of a course assigned by a committee which uses guidelines provided by the United States Golf Association.

Cup

The plastic or metal lining of the hole on the putting green. It is 4¼" in diameter and at least 4" deep.

Cut Shot
A stroke which gives the ball a clockwise spin and causes it to curve from left to right.

Divot
A piece of turf which is displaced by a player's club. It should be replaced and patted down.

Dogleg
A hole with a fairway which bends to the right or to the left.

Dormie
A situation in match play in which a player or a team is leading by as many holes as there are holes remaining.

Double Bogey
A score of two strokes over par on a hole.

Double Eagle
A score of three strokes under par on a hole.

Down
The number of holes a player or a side is behind in a match.

Draw
A shot which curves slightly to the left.

Drive
A shot made from the teeing ground.

Driver
The #1 wood club.

Dub
A poor shot or a poorly skilled golfer.

Duffer
A poor golfer. Also sometimes called a "hacker."

Eagle
A score of two strokes under par on a hole.

Explosion
A shot from a sand bunker in which the clubhead slides under the ball and displaces a fairly large amount of sand.

Fade
A shot which curves slightly to the right.

Fairway

The mowed area of the golf course between the teeing ground and the putting green.

Fat Shot

A stroke in which the ground is struck before the ball.

Fellow Competitor

The term used in the United States Golf Association rules to refer to a person with whom you play in stroke competition.

Flagstick

The movable pole in the hole with a flag attached to the top. Also called the pin.

Flat Swing

A swing which is less upright and more shallow than the normal swing.

Follow-Through

The part of the swing after the clubface has contacted the ball.

Fore

A warning which is shouted to anyone in danger of being hit by a golf ball. An old English word.

Foursome

The common term for four players playing in a group. Technically, it describes a match in which two partners play against another team of two, each playing one ball, stroking alternately.

Forward Press

A slight movement toward the target of some part of the body prior to the backswing.

Frog Hair

See *apron*.

Gimmie

A slang expression for a conceded putt in match play.

Gowf

The Scottish word for striking with the hand. Some historians claim that golf probably originated from this term.

Grain

The direction is which flat-lying grass grows on a putting green.

Green

The putting surface, which is a closely cut area of the course.

Grip

The upper portion of the club shaft. Also the player's grasp of the club.

Gross Score

The player's actual score on a hole or a round, with no handicap strokes deducted.

Ground

Touching the ground with the sole of the club at address. This is not allowed in a hazard.

Ground Under Repair

Designated areas on a golf course which allow for free drop outside those areas.

Halved

A term used to designate a tied hole in match play.

Handicap

A number which indicates a golfer's skill. It is based upon the difference between the actual scores a player shoots and the course ratings of the courses on which the scores were made. It provides a way for players of different abilities to play on a fairly equal basis.

Hazard

According to the United States Golf Association rules, a designation for a bunker (sand trap) , water area, or water hazard.

Head

The striking part of the club at the lower end of the shaft.

Heel

The part of the clubface nearest the shaft.

High Side

The area above the hole on a sloping green.

Hole High

A ball which is even with the hole but off to one side.

Hole Out

To stroke the ball into the cup.

Honor

The privilege of shooting first from the teeing ground.

Hood

A closed clubface. Tilting the top edge of the club forward, thus decreasing the loft.

Hook

A shot which curves in flight from right to left.

Hosel

The extension of the head of the club into which the shaft fits.

In

The designation on a score card for the second nine holes of an eighteen-hole course.

Inside-Out

The clubhead moves across the intended line of flight from left to right during impact.

Inside The Line

As the player addresses and swings at the ball, this is the area on the player's side of the intended line of flight.

Intended Line

The path along which the player plans to hit the shot. Also referred to as the "target line."

Interlock or Interlocking

A type of grip in which the left forefinger and right little finger are intertwined.

Irons

The clubs whose heads are made primarily of metal, not including the putter.

Kolf

The Dutch word meaning club. Some historians say golf originated from this word.

LPGA
The Ladies Professional Golf Association.

Lag
Putting with the intention of ending close to the hole.

Lateral Water Hazard
A water hazard which runs parallel or almost parallel to the line of play on a hole.

Lie
The position of the ball on the course. Also refers to the angle formed by the sole of the club and the shaft.

Links
A term which refers to that which is built over sandy soil deposited by ocean tides ("linked to the seas"). Today a term used synonymously with golf course.

Lip
The edge of the hole. Also a putt which rims the hole but does not go in.

Loft
The backward slant or angle of the clubface. Also, to cause the ball to rise into the air.

Loose Impediment
A natural object not fixed or growing, such as pebbles, leaves, and twigs.

Low Side
The area below the hole on a slanted green.

Mashie
A hickory-shafted iron club approximately like the current #5 iron.

Match Play
Competition based on the number of holes won or lost rather than on strokes.

Medal
The lowest of all of the qualifying scores. The person shooting this score is the medalist.

Medal Play
The common term given to stroke play.

Mid-Iron

A hickory-shafted club like the current #2 iron.

Mulligan

In friendly competition, an illegal second shot from the first tee if the first shot is a poor one. Named after a Canadian, Dr. David Mulligan.

Nassau

A type of scoring in which three points are given: one for each nine holes and one for the eighteen holes.

Net Score

The score for a hole or for a round after the player's handicap has been deducted from the gross score.

Niblick

A club somewhat like the current #9 iron.

Obstruction

Usually refers to anything on the course which is artificial, whether fixed or movable. See United States Golf Association rules for exceptions.

Open Face

The clubhead is aimed right of the intended line of flight.

Open Stance

The right foot is closer than the left foot to the intended line of flight.

Open Tournament

Competition which allows the entry of both amateurs and professionals.

Opponent

The opposing player in match play.

Out Of Bounds

An area usually marked by stakes, a fence, or a wall which is outside of the course proper. Play in this area is prohibited.

Out

The designation for the first nine holes of an eighteen-hole course.

Outside-In
Movement of the clubhead from right to left across the intended line of flight.

Overlap or Overlapping
The grip in which the right little finger laps over the left forefinger.

Par
The score a skilled player is expected to make on a hole. This score allows for two putts.

PGA
The Men's Professional Golf Association.

Pin High
See *hole high.*

Pitch
An approach shot with a high trajectory which stops relatively fast after landing.

Play Through
An invitation given by slower players to let the group behind them go ahead.

Preferred Lie
An easing of the rules which permits the players to move the ball to a better position in the fairway when course conditions are poor. Also called "winter rules."

Provisional Ball
A second ball which is hit before a player looks for an original ball which might be lost or out of bounds.

Press
Using more force than necessary or attempting to stroke beyond one's own ability.

Pull
A shot which travels on a fairly straight line to the left of the intended target.

Push
A shot which travels on a fairly straight line to the right of the intended target.

Putter

The least-lofted club, which is usually used only on the putting green.

Putting Green

See *green*.

Rough

An area which has fairly long grass. It is not considered fairway, hazard, or green.

Rub Of The Green

A term used for the situation in which a shot is stopped or deflected by an outside agency.

Sand Trap

See *bunker.*

Scotch Foursome

Common term for a foursome in which two teams compete, each team using only one ball and hitting it alternately.

Scratch Player

A player who has a handicap of zero and who plays consistently close to par.

Setup

See *address*.

Shaft

The long portion of the club to which the grip and clubhead are attached.

Slice

A shot which curves sharply from left to right of the intended line of flight.

Sole

The bottom of the clubhead.

Shank

A shot which goes sharply to the right after being contacted on the neck or hosel of the club.

Spoon

The #3 wood.

Stance

The position of the feet in the address of the ball.

Square Face

The clubhead is aimed at the intended line of flight at the address.

Square Stance

Both feet are the same distance from the intended line of flight.

Stiff

A shot which finished very close to the flagstick.

Stroke Play

Competition based upon the total strokes taken by a player or a side.

Sudden Death

Extra holes played by players tied at the end of competition until a winner is determined.

Summer Rules

The official rules of golf which require the player to play the ball as it lies.

Takeaway

The initial part of the backswing.

Target Line

The imaginary line which extends from the player's target back to, through, and beyond the ball.

Tee

The small wooden peg from which the ball is played on the teeing ground.

Teeing Ground

A rectangular area defined by markers, which is no more than two club lengths in depth. The first shot of every hole is played from here and is commonly called the "tee."

Texas Wedge

A slang term which refers to the putter when it is used for shots from off the putting green.

Through The Green

A designation for the whole area of the course except the teeing ground and the green of the hole being played, and including all hazards.

Tight Lie

A ball which is well down in the grass or very close to the surface being played.

Toe

The part of the clubhead farthest from the shaft.

Top

A shot in which the ball is contacted above its center.

Unplayable Lie

A ball (not in a water hazard) which is determined to be unplayable by its owner.

USGA

The United States Golf Association, the governing body of golf in the United States. Organized in 1894.

Waggle

Clubhead movement at the time of address and prior to the swing.

Whiff

A miss. A stroke in which no contact is made with the ball.

Winter Rules

See *preferred lie*.

Woods

The clubs which have heads made primarily of wood.

SUGGESTED READINGS

Charles, Bob. *Left-Handed Golf.*
  Norwalk, CT: Golf Digest, Inc., 1965.
Flick, Jim, and Aultman, Dick. *Square to Square Golf in Pictures.*
  Norwalk, CT: Golf Digest, Inc., 1974.
Grout, Jack, and Aultman, Dick. *Let Me Teach You Golf As I Taught Jack Nicklaus.*
  New York: Atheneum, 1977.
Kemp, Charles F. *The World of Golf and the Game of Life.*
  St. Louis: Bethany Press, 1978.
Morley, David C. *The Missing Links: Golf and the Mind.*
  New York: Grosset & Dunlap, 1976.
Nelson, Byron. *Shape Your Swing the Modern Way.*
  Norwalk, CT: Golf Digest, Inc., 1976.
Nicklaus, Jack. *Jack Nicklaus' Lesson Tee.*
  Norwalk, CT: Golf Digest, Inc., 1977.
Obitz, Harry, and Farley, Dick. *Six Days to Better Golf.*
  New York: Harper & Row, 1977.
Stewart, Earl, and Gun, Harry E. *Left-Handers' Golf Book.*
  Matteson, IL: Great Lakes Living Press, 1976.
Toski, Bob, and Aultman, Dick. *The Touch System for Better Golf.*
  Norwalk, CT: Golf Digest, Inc., 1978.
Toski, Bob, and Flick, Jim. *How to Become a Complete Golfer.*
  Norwalk, CT: Golf Digest, Inc., 1978.

PERIODICALS

Golf Magazine.
  Published monthly by Times Mirror Magazines, Inc., New York, NY.
Golf Digest.
  Published monthly by Golf Digest, Inc., Norwalk, CT.

RULE BOOKS

United States Golf Association, *The Rules of Golf.*
  Published each year, available from United States Golf Association Golf House, Far Hills, NJ 07931.
United States Golf Association, *Golf Rules in Pictures.*
  New York: Grosset & Dunlap, 1977.
National Golf Foundation, *Easy Way to Learn Golf Rules.*
  200 Castlewood Street, North Palm Beach, FL. 33408.